D0742779

violence

violence

THE CRISIS OF AMERICAN CONFIDENCE

EDITED BY HUGH DAVIS GRAHAM

ASSOCIATE EDITORS STEPHEN PAUL MAHINKA

AND DEAN WILLIAM RUDOY

THE JOHNS HOPKINS PRESS · BALTIMORE AND LONDON

The Johns Hopkins Press, Baltimore, Maryland 21218
The Johns Hopkins Press Ltd., London

Library of Congress Catalog Card Number 79-171554
ISBN 0-8018-1299-2 (cloth)
ISBN 0-8018-1328-X (paper)

CONTENTS

v

ACKNOWLEDGMENTS

For their assistance and support in organizing The Milton S. Eisenhower Symposium 1970 at The Johns Hopkins University, the editors would like to thank Peter D. W. Heberling and Richard L. Posen. For their essential help with manuscript preparation, we would like to thank Alice A. Anderson and Catherine Schonberg.

PREFACE

THIS VOLUME CONTAINS the addresses of twelve of the participants
in the Milton S. Eisenhower Symposium 1970, the original title
of which was "The United States in the 1970s: Perspectives on
Violence." The Eisenhower Symposium was inaugurated in 1967
by the student council of The Johns Hopkins University as a tribute to Dr. Eisenhower for his exceptional service to the Hopkins
community during his tenure as president of the university from
1956 to 1967. Each year since its initiation the symposium, hoping
to inspire thought and discussion in areas of vital concern, has
presented distinguished speakers on national and international
issues. As co-chairmen of the Eisenhower Symposium 1970, we
chose the topic of domestic violence in light of the crisis of violence facing this society. The participants in the symposium were
noted authorities on the origins and control of American violence but
reflect a wide spectrum of views on this salient issue.

All of the addresses have been revised for publication. The Introduction and Overview, a carefully documented and sobering

analysis of group violence and the dimensions of our contemporary wave of violent crime, was prepared by Dr. Milton S. Eisenhower, who was chairman of the National Commission on the Causes and Prevention of Violence.[1] Part I contains Professor Henry Steele Commager's extensive interpretation of the history of American violence. Part II presents the analyses of four prominent men who view the problem of criminal violence from the perspectives of the dominant institutions that must deal with the problem: for the courts, Earl Warren, former Chief Justice of the U.S. Supreme Court; for the Congress, Representative Gerald R. Ford of Michigan; for the presidency, Herbert G. Klein, White House director of communications; and for the police, Quinn Tamm, who is executive director of the International Association of Chiefs of Police.

Part III focuses more broadly on the relations of individual and group violence to American society and especially to our political life. Dr. Jerome Frank, professor of psychiatry at The Johns Hopkins School of Medicine, assesses the hereditary and environmental dimensions of the psychology of violence. Judge A. Leon Higginbotham, vice-chairman of the National Commission on the Causes and Prevention of Violence, views the recent burgeoning of prison riots, especially among black prisoners, as an alarming bellwether of fundamental social crisis. David Brinkley, the television newscaster, attacks both the unresponsive rigidities of America's major institutions—especially the federal government—and the suicidal naïveté of young revolutionaries who cannot win and who invite only a rightist repression. In a lively and occasionally searing debate, the philosopher Charles Frankel of Columbia University assaults most of the case for civil disobedience and the historian Howard Zinn of Boston University paints a devastating portrait of the systematic and dehumanizing inequities that have masqueraded as the "rule of law" in American life. Both speakers clash even more directly and personally in spirited rejoinders. The volume concludes with John Gardner's call for a national citizens' lobby to revitalize and restructure our failing institutions.

[1] On April 5, 1971, Dr. Eisenhower assumed the duties of interim president of The Johns Hopkins University.

This volume is entitled *Violence: The Crisis of American Confidence* because a prominent theme throughout the symposium was alarm that our historically sanctified institutions were now failing us—that our social fabric was being torn apart and that our traditional "optimistic fatalism" was suddenly irrelevant, even dangerous. We must ask, what are the *structural* origins of social conflict? It is possible that they may largely be found in the dominance relations,[2] or the hierarchy of power, existing in American society. If this is true, then some extremely difficult structural readjustments may be necessary before we may hope to see an abatement of violence in America. Too many groups in our society are denied a reasonable degree of influence and power for us to expect that palliative measures alone will suffice.

The editor of this volume, Hugh Davis Graham, has previously observed that historically one group in our society, the Anglo-Americans, "have used their access to the levers of power to maintain their dominance, using legal force surrounded by an aura of legitimacy."[3] It is just this limitation of access to other groups, this closure of the opportunity to influence decisions that may decisively affect their own lives, that is increasingly impossible to tolerate in the United States. The crucial question, then, seems to be how best to open the system to a more equitable distribution of power.

In this connection, it is important to remember that America has experienced periodic episodes of serious mass violence involving disadvantaged groups in pursuit of all manner of political, social, and economic objectives. Contrary to popular opinion, the history of America has been fraught with violence. The concept of peaceful progress is indeed a myth if one means by it "that the established order is self-transforming, or that groups in positions of power will always share power with outsiders without being threat-

---

[2] See Ralf Dahrendorf, "Towards a Theory of Social Conflict," *Journal of Conflict Resolution*, 11 (1958): 177 ff.

[3] Hugh Davis Graham and Ted Robert Gurr, "Conclusion," in Graham and Gurr (eds.), *The History of Violence in America* (New York: Frederick A. Praeger, 1969), p. 794.

ened by actual or potential violence."[4] It may be that in the absence of extensive public support or at least public acquiescence the resort to violence will not achieve one's objectives. The point is neither that violence always works nor that it always fails but rather, as Richard Rubenstein has observed, "that political and economic power is not as easily shared or turned over to powerless outsiders, as has been thought."[5]

One of the main reasons why this is so, in addition to human imperfection, is the organizational structure of modern American society. To say that our bureaucratic institutions have become increasingly unresponsive and often uncontrollable is commonplace. What it means in light of the accelerating velocity of social change, however, is that the machinery of our society is no longer operating in a manner that will allow us to solve our major problems. As members of a generation profoundly dissatisfied with the intensely slow responses of our inherited institutions to critical problems, we share the feeling of social malaise, the loss of confidence that is reflected to varying degrees in all the following contributions.

It is this lack of a sense of mastery of one's own destiny, this feeling of drift and powerlessness, that is perhaps the root cause of violence in America. To the degree that this is true, then, as John Gardner wrote recently, "the crucial task is to design a society (and institutions) capable of continuous change, continuous renewal, continuous responsiveness."[6] Only then will violence become unnecessary to bring about social change. Such far-reaching institutional change may be a utopian vision; if so, in the midst of the present crisis of America's social order we may have to accept some kinds of violence as legitimate indicators of areas where change is vitally necessary.

Indeed, a thorough taking of stock like that presented here, with its implicit reassessment of values, priorities, and directions, could constitute a healthy and essential prelude to fundamental social

[4] Richard E. Rubenstein, *Rebels in Eden: Mass Political Violence in the United States* (Boston: Little, Brown, 1970), p. 9.

[5] *Ibid.*, p. 18.

[6] John W. Gardner, *The Recovery of Confidence* (New York: W. W. Norton, 1970), p. 25.

and institutional change. These leaders do not agree on precisely what the new directions should be, but their analyses are not devoid of constructive suggestions and cautious hope. Perhaps only from such a dialogue can a new vision spring.

The urgent need for a new vision was eloquently expressed by Senator Robert F. Kennedy, who spoke of the necessity for a change of values and attitudes on the part of all Americans. He condemned "the violence of institutions—indifference, inaction, and decay. This is the violence," he continued, "that afflicts the poor, that poisons relations between men because their skin has different colors. . . . For when you teach a man to hate and to fear his brother—when you teach that he is a lesser man because of his color or his beliefs or the policies that he pursues—when you teach that those who differ from you threaten your freedom, or your job, or your home, or your family, then you also learn to confront others, not as fellow citizens, but as enemies to be met not with cooperation but with conquest, to be subjugated, to be mastered. We learn to share only a common fear—only a common desire to retreat from each other—only a common impulse to meet disagreement with force. For all this there are no final answers for those of us who are American citizens. Yet we know what we must do, and that is to achieve true justice among all of our fellow citizens."[7]

Our task in facing the crisis of violence in America, then, is to recognize the injustices and inequities within our society and to commit ourselves to the quest for true justice and equality among all our people. The quest has been long delayed; to neglect it further in this critical period may irrevocably damage our nation.

Baltimore, Maryland   Stephen Paul Mahinka
                                        Dean William Rudoy

---

[7] Robert F. Kennedy, Cleveland, April 5, 1968, following the assassination of Dr. Martin Luther King, Jr., from a Columbia record, *Robert Francis Kennedy: A Memorial*, D2S792.

milton s. eisenhower

INTRODUCTION AND OVERVIEW

WE LIVE IN AN URBAN SOCIETY. We live in an affluent society. And we live in a society that is violent. In the convergence of those three characteristics lies a central problem for America in the 1970s.

These three characteristics are not new to our history. Our nation was born in violent revolution, expanded to the Pacific with the sword as well as the plow, and was violently redeemed from the sin of slavery by the Civil War. The face of violence is always ugly, and if violence attended the birth, expansion, and preserva-

Milton S. Eisenhower is president emeritus and acting president of The Johns Hopkins University. He was formerly president of Kansas State University and Pennsylvania State University. His extensive involvement in American governmental affairs, which began in 1924, includes diplomatic appointments and service in the Department of Agriculture, in the Office of War Information, with UNESCO, and on numerous governmental commissions. Most recently he was chairman of the National Commission on the Causes and Prevention of Violence, 1968–69. His publications include *The Wine Is Bitter: The United States and Latin America* (Garden City, N.Y.: Doubleday, 1963).

tion of our Union, it has also pervaded our vigilantism, our race riots and lynchings, our labor strife and, more than we have cared to admit, our politics and processes of government. But if violence is not new to America, never before have so many Americans lived in the metropolis and never before have we been so affluent. Yet our violence persists and intensifies, bringing with it its constant companion: fear.

The historical roots of our legacy of violence are traced and analyzed by Professor Commager in Part I of this volume, and in Part III the broad social sources, implications, and consequences of our contemporary violence, both criminal and collective, are surveyed and debated from a variety of professional and public perspectives by recognized authorities in American life. I propose in this discussion to present, both as a general introduction and especially as prelude to Part II, a substantive and personal assessment of that alarmingly growing form of violence that is gnawing at the essential optimism of the American spirit: violent crime.

In the metropolitan areas, where two-thirds of the American people live, violent crime is rising, and fear is rising in its wake. Fear is manifested in the locked doors, the empty streets, the growing number of guns bought for self-protection, the signs on public buses that say "Driver does not carry cash." It is the neglected conditions in American cities that help to account for the rise in violent crime, but violent crime is the cancer that may kill the cities and paralyze the suburbs as well.

The potential achievements of American affluence—flights to other planets, supersonic transports, rebuilt cities, effective systems of mass transit, clean air and water—all will be hollow if, while reaching them, we ignore the despair and alienation of a large portion of our citizens who do not share adequately in America's affluence. The price of ignoring their situation will be ever-mounting rates of violent crime—and ever-spreading fear, with its paralyzing results.

Dr. Norval Morris, professor of law and criminology at the University of Chicago, said to the Commission on Violence, "Crime for the first time is a threat to the quality of life in this country." And Dr. Price M. Cobbs, the distinguished psychiatrist, said, "If violence continues at its present pace, we may well witness the end of the grand experiment of democracy." The Commission on the Causes and Prevention of Violence, after obtaining the unprecedented help of 200 of the nation's leading scholars in history, law, sociology, criminology, psychiatry, and other fields; after obtaining public evidence from some 150 individuals ranging from student radicals to police chiefs, from scholars to the head of the Federal Bureau of Investigation; and after considering this complex problem among ourselves for a year and a half, said to the President of the United States: "We solemnly declare our conviction that this nation is entering a period in which our people need to be as concerned by the internal dangers to our free society as by any possible combination of external threats."

The best estimate of the number of serious crimes committed in the United States each year is 10 million, of which more than 1.2 million are violent crimes: homicides, aggravated assaults, forcible rapes, and robberies. According to another estimate, more than 1 out of 100 Americans commits a major violent crime in any one year. Many more, of course, commit a serious crime some time in their lives.

This violence in our midst earns us the distinction of being the clear leader in violent crime among the modern, stable nations of the world. Thus the United States, with 200 million people, averages *fifty* times as many gun murders a year as do England, Germany, and Japan combined, with their total population of 214 million.

This appalling statistic calls to mind other salient features of our culture. The 100 million firearms privately owned by Americans give us the distinction of having by far the highest gun-to-population ratio of any nation on earth. About half of all American homes have a firearm, and many have more than one. More than 25 million of those weapons are *concealable handguns*, and these are the firearms used in virtually all aggravated assaults and robberies involving firearms and in three-fourths of all gun murders.

Parenthetically, let me add that I continue to be perplexed by the blind, emotional resistance that greets any proposal to bring this senseless excess under control. We lag behind every other civilized nation in the world in failing to have a comprehensive, effective national policy of firearms control. Yet when the Commission on Violence, after careful weighing of all the relevant facts and arguments, recommended a policy of restrictive licensing of handguns and a simple identification system for long guns, vitriolic mail began to pour into my office. I was labeled with every epithet I'd ever heard—and some I'd never heard before—from "you shame the Eisenhower name" to "fascist" and even to "communist" (these last two covering quite a spectrum). Vociferous opposition of this sort has kept this nation from instituting a sane, effective policy of firearms control. In the meantime, the senseless tragedies repeat themselves: the domestic quarrel or argument between friends turns into a homicide because a gun is available for acting on the rage. Guns are handy to support the yearnings of the sex maniac. Guns are available to those who hold up banks, filling stations, savings and loan associations—and too often the guns are used as more than a threat. So merchants are leaving the city in fear of their lives. Residents are fleeing to the suburbs and there installing every known type of protective device. And in the meantime, police in most parts of the country are without an effective legal maneuver against the criminal who possesses a pistol unless they catch him in the actual act of using it in a crime.

If, on the other hand, we had restrictive licensing of handguns similar to the Sullivan law of New York State, police could, with the use of modern electronic equipment, spot a metallic object on a suspect and, even under recent Supreme Court rulings, frisk him.

If the suspect is found with a gun and lacks a license, he can be convicted and sentenced on that evidence alone. There can be no doubt that in a few years the right law would have a·profound effect in reducing the crimes of armed robbery, aggravated assault, and homicide.

Guns alone do not give us the distinction of being the most violent of the advanced societies of the world. Controlling firearms would greatly reduce fatalities and discourage many criminal careers, but international comparisons show that our capacity for acts of rage and rapacity is impressive, whether or not firearms are involved. Thus aggravated assault, which often is just a murder that didn't work out, occurs in the United States at a rate twice that of England and Wales, eighteen times that of Canada. Rape occurs at a rate three times that of Canada, twelve times that of England and Wales. Our robbery rate is double that of Canada, nine times that of England and Wales.

To complete the picture of America the Violent we would have to sketch in the riots that have erupted in American cities in recent years, the firebombings of campus and public buildings by a lunatic radical minority, the attacks by mobs on peaceful demonstrators, and the outrageous killings of students by law enforcement personnel.

By cold statistics, group violence has not been a major problem compared to individual acts of violent crime. A Commission on Violence study looked back over five years and counted 190 deaths and 9,100 injuries from group violence, mostly ghetto riots. In that same five-year period 53,000 Americans were victims of reported murders and more than a million were injured in aggravated assaults. If it is fair to extrapolate from a Harris poll conducted for the commission, 62 million Americans have been punched or beaten at some point in their lives and 24 million have been threatened with a gun or actually shot at.

While group violence is the secondary problem, its prevalence and high visibility in contemporary America does help to shape attitudes which encourage violent crime—a matter I will return to in a moment.

We will have to look at the picture of violence in America more closely to see where violent crime is concentrated if we are to begin to understand its causes and know where to invest our social resources to reduce its incidence. The National Commission on Violence found:

First, that violent crime is heavily concentrated in the larger cities. There the rate of crime per unit of population is eight times the rural rate, six times the smaller town rate. The twenty-six cities with more than half a million residents each account for only a sixth of our nation's population but almost a half of our total reported violent crimes. If you live in a metropolitan area today your mathematical chances of becoming a victim of a homicide, a rape, an assault, or a robbery are 1 in 125 *each year*. If you live in the city of Baltimore, as I do, your mathematical chance of becoming a victim of one of these four violent crimes is 1 in 49 each year. So the odds are *in favor* of a Baltimore resident's becoming a victim of a violent crime during his lifetime.

Second, violent crime in cities is overwhelmingly committed by males.

Third, violent crime in cities is concentrated among youthful offenders. By far the highest urban arrest rate for homicide occurs in the fifteen to twenty-four age group. For rape, robbery, and aggravated assault, arrests in the fifteen to twenty-four group are three times as high as for any other age group. There have been disturbing increases in arrest rates among youngsters ten to fourteen—an increase of 300 percent in assaults and 200 percent in robberies between 1958 and 1967.

Fourth, violent crime in the cities is committed primarily by individuals at the lower end of the socioeconomic scale.

Fifth, violent crime in the cities stems disproportionately from the ghetto slums where most Negroes live. Where discrimination is added to low socioeconomic status, in other words, crime rates are especially high. To describe violent crime as primarily a ghetto phenomenon is to make a statement about social and cultural conditions, not about racial characteristics. I emphasize that all evidence indicates that one race is no more criminogenic than another. Professor Marvin Wolfgang, the eminent sociologist and criminologist who served as codirector of research for the Commission on Violence, recently published a book on this subject. Solid research conducted over a long period of years shows no correlation between race and crime. The correlation is between the total environmental and human conditions in which some people live and crime.

Sixth, the victims of violent crimes in the cities generally have the same characteristics as the offenders—that is, they tend to be males, youths, poor persons, and blacks. Against the dangerous myth that violent crime is a kind of interracial warfare, I cite the fact that nine out of ten urban homicides, aggravated assaults, and rapes involve victims and offenders of the same race. An exception is robbery. Our studies showed that 45 percent of urban robberies involves Negroes robbing whites—very often young black males robbing somewhat older white males.

Seventh, except for robbery, violent crimes tend to be acts of passion among intimates and acquaintances. This is true in almost half the cases of rape and the great majority of assaults and homicides. Robbery, on the other hand, is committed by a stranger eight times out of ten.

Finally, by far the greatest proportion of all serious violence is committed by repeaters. In a study of 10,000 boys in Philadelphia, 627—only 6 percent of those studied—accounted for 53 percent of the homicides, rapes, and assaults known to the police and 71 percent of the robberies.

In sum, violent crime in the cities is committed primarily by males rather than females, by youths rather than older people, by the poor and unskilled rather than the more successful, and by ghetto blacks rather than residents of more affluent sections of the city. The highest rates of violent crime occur in the population where these characteristics all intersect: the young, poor Negro male.

I add the caveat that violent crime is not exclusively a province of ghetto youth. Alcoholics and drug addicts who are a danger to their fellow citizens come from all strata of society. The thin shell of civility that houses our aggressive impulses has been known to crack open and spill violence in some of the so-called finest families in America. On the other hand, the social pathology that exists in the ghetto does not turn all poor, young Negro males, nor even a majority of them, into criminals.

We need to focus our attention on the inner city ghetto because that is where the major problem of violent crime exists. That is where the socially destructive forces are at work breeding violent crime, which hastens the decay of our cities, which in turn breeds more crime. There are certain dispositions in American thinking that tend to block our understanding of ghetto problems. We are a hard-working people. We believe hard work is important because we believe success—however we choose to define it—is the inevitable reward for hard work. We tend to regard as morally inferior those who are failures. We tend to say they have only themselves to blame.

We tend also to forget how, for hundreds of years, the realities of American life have made a cruel mockery of the work-for-your-reward ethic for the black segment of our population. We boast of what our immigrant ancestors were able to accomplish while ignoring the fact that their assimilation came easier because they were the "right" color. We forget that they came from Europe with some skills and at a time when industry thrived on labor, not science and technology, and welcomed all the white workers it could get. We forget that the white immigrant ghettos had their high rates of crime until they were assimilated into the larger society, a process that often required several generations. Indeed, the success of white immigrants still isn't all we boast it to be; there are still twice as many whites living below the poverty line as non-whites.

Many who acknowledge that blacks have been pounded to despair by discrimination, and many who don't, assume that Negro parents do not bother to discipline their children and take no interest in their moral development. Yet as Robert Coles, the prominent Harvard psychiatrist, has pointed out, "Negro children probably receive more punitively enforced reminders of what is right and wrong than any other segment of our population." But consider how hollow the maternal admonitions begin to sound once the realities of the ghetto start to impinge on a black youngster's awareness. Like every American mother she says, "Work hard in school; it's the only way to get ahead." What measure of reality does that have for the ghetto youth? There are few or no examples of educated, successful men in his immediate experiences. His father, if he has one, and the men up and down the block sweat at menial and intermittent jobs. The one across the street with the fancy convertible isn't working for the sanitation department; he's pushing drugs or robbing corner grocery stores.

In the crowded apartment there are no quiet places for study, no books or serious magazines, no conversations to stimulate the intellect. On the other hand, there is the constant lure of the television set. The average young ghetto resident, by the time he is eighteen, will have spent more time watching television than in school. There is also the lure of the street where the other children are running and playing, often deep into the night, and where a youngster may have to engage in crime or the use of dope to be accepted by his peers. This is what Professor Wolfgang calls the subculture of violence. The neighborhood school, dilapidated and poorly equipped, has accommodated itself to defeat. It asks only for a modicum of discipline, ignores the strivings of eager students and the indifference of rebellious students, and automatically promotes to the next higher grade every student just so it can have room for the next crop of undereducated and unmotivated children.

If the ghetto youth has the determination to swim against the tides all the way to a high school diploma—and, of course, many do not—he may find job or further educational opportunities waiting for him. In the past few years, barriers to advancement for high-school-educated blacks have been falling. If he drops out, as so many do, he may find the doors to meaningful job opportunities closed to him. In the American value system he is now a full-fledged failure, and he is quite aware of it. All those material comforts displayed and advertised on the television screen are not to be his—at least not by legitimate means.

And why not use violence to get what he needs to be somebody? He has little to gain by playing according to society's rules and little to lose by not. He is familiar with violence. In the disintegrated community of the ghetto, violent quarrels, brawls, and careers in crime are commonplace. Violence is also a way of proving manliness, especially in the street gangs of the inner city. The larger society apparently does not find violence abhorrent. Violence is a constant theme in television dramas and is touted in American folklore. Americans love their guns; they have, as I have said, the highest gun-to-population ratio of any nation in the world. Considering the pressures, frustrations, and temptations at work on the youth in our ghettos, the wonder is that violent crime rates in the cities are not higher than they are.

Yet conditions in the ghettos have been improving. During this past decade incomes of Negroes in cities increased, the percentage of blacks completing high school rose as did the percentage entering universities, and unemployment rates dropped significantly. We are faced with an apparent paradox: while conditions have been improving for inner-city blacks, rates of violent crime among them have been soaring. As closely as the Commission on Violence could determine, the combined rate of violent crimes per unit of population has increased 100 percent during the last ten years.

A partial answer to this paradox is that real gains for blacks have still left significant gaps between their conditions and those of whites. Thus, for example, the Negro unemployment rate continues to be about twice that for whites. And unemployment among black teenagers in cities has actually been increasing. Last year it stood at 25 percent, which was two and a half times the unemployment rate for white teenagers.

Second, demographic changes in this country would lead one to expect an increase in violent crime. The age group most involved in violent crime, fifteen to twenty-four, has soared both in number and proportion of the total population, from 20 million ten years ago to 29 million today and from 11 percent of the population to almost 15 percent. The increasing urbanization of our society also helps to account for the rise in violent crime. Actually the spectacular growth in the past ten years has taken place in the suburbs. Middle class, mostly affluent whites, have been moving out of the cities, leaving them increasingly to the poor, black population, which suffers inadequate services financed by a declining tax base. Another demographic trend of some bearing is the increasing instability of American families. Divorces and separations are on the rise in every segment of the population, but nowhere as spectacularly as among poor blacks in our cities. Ten years ago half of the poor black children in the central cities lived with both parents. Today only 22 percent of the children in that category live with both—a sad circumstance that should have been improved, not permitted to grow worse. This is probably a major consequence of our anachronistic welfare system.

A third factor has been a vast increase in the number of firearms in private hands. Sales of long guns, the Commission on Violence found, doubled from 1962 to 1968. In the same period sales of handguns quadrupled.

Fourth, we are living in a time of profound changes—technological, occupational, social, and cultural. Times of great change alter how we work, think, and live. They set us adrift from our moorings and create tensions and uncertainties. If American parents seem unduly permissive, if they appear to be unsure about the values to encourage in their children and the standards to impose, perhaps it is because American society has already changed greatly since their own childhood and is destined to change even more in the future. In the absence of clear-cut expectations and standards the traditional social controls have lost their grip, and violence is one result of the breakdown. This may explain why violence is rising among youth in affluent middle class homes, as well as in the ghettos.

A fifth and related change is that events in the 1960s have served to diminish the respect accorded the institutions of government. The spectacle of governors defying federal court orders, of policemen beating demonstrators, of mobs looting stores with impunity, of some college students destroying property and then demanding amnesty, of elected officials exposed in corruption—all these, and more, have served to encourage a cynical disrespect for law and law-making institutions.

Besides encouraging the attitude that lawful behavior is "just for suckers," such events tend to give direct legitimacy to violence. The deep divisions within our country set off tensions and anger, but the readiness with which some groups give violent expression to their anger and impatience creates an appealing, contagious, but very dangerous model. Urban riots had a powerful lesson for ghetto youth: that it is perfectly all right to vent one's dissatisfactions in acts of violence. More recently, violence—as distinguished, of course, from peaceful protest or demonstration—on the nation's campuses has probably had an effect even more powerful. If the most privileged young people can have their violent donnybrooks, a ghetto youth is entitled to ask, why shouldn't I?

Of course the frustrations of ghetto life are very real. They have been especially deep in recent years because of the so-called revolution of rising expectations. Life for Americans generally has grown more comfortable and rewarding, there have been noticeable improvements for the poor, but improvements in the ghetto have not kept pace with the political promises or with what the poor and disadvantaged have come to expect. It is hardly surprising that the resulting frustrations give rise to violent crime.

There remains one very obvious reason for mounting crime in our society: the increasing failure of law enforcement agencies to cope with it. Consider the grim statistics. Probably 10 million serious crimes were committed in the United States last year. About half of these crimes were never reported to the Federal Bureau of Investigation. Only 12 percent of those 10 million crimes resulted in the arrest of anyone. Only 6 percent resulted in the conviction of anyone, and this 6 percent included many pleas to lesser offenses. Only 1½ percent resulted in the incarceration of anyone. And of those who were incarcerated, most will return to prison another time for additional offenses. As Lloyd Cutler, eminent lawyer and executive director of the Violence Commission, remarked on these statistics: "It would be hard to argue that crime does not pay. The sad fact is that our criminal justice system, as presently operated, does not deter, does not detect, does not convict, and does not correct." As crimes go unpunished and as criminals go through the corrections system changed for the worse instead of the better, it is no wonder that crime is on the increase.

Police departments in American cities are understaffed and underequipped. Police are undereducated and undertrained. Juvenile courts have failed to live up to their humane ideal. The lower courts in which most adults are tried too often have crowded dockets, inadequate procedures for investigating the defendant and circumstances, and necessarily shoddy ways of dispensing justice. The jails in which indigent defendants sit awaiting trial have been aptly described as "rabbit warrens." Prisons have earned the label "schools for criminals." Inside prison walls are terrorist societies ruled more by prisoners themselves than by guards. Lacking equipment and sufficient professional staff, prison training programs are outmoded and rehabilitation services are wholly inadequate. At the end of their terms, most prisoners are thrust out on the street without meaningful help in readjustment.

The Crime Commission studied the deplorable conditions of our criminal justice system and, in its 1967 report, made dozens of thoughtful recommendations for improving all its aspects—police, courts, corrections. The National Commission on Violence added a few recommendations of its own, mostly having to do with improving coordination among the various agencies of the system. We recommended that urban governments form offices of criminal justice to improve coordination at the local level. We urged citizens to form advisory groups in local areas to help with that effort. We suggested that leading citizens be invited to form a privately financed National Citizens Justice Center to encourage improvements in the criminal justice system at all levels, through private citizens' groups as well as government agencies.

This is not the occasion for detailing further the recommendations of either commission. But I do want to call your attention to one additional recommendation of the Violence Commission: that we as a nation "give concrete expression to our concern about crime by a solemn national commitment to double our investment in the administration of justice as rapidly as such an investment can be wisely planned and utilized." At present, our entire criminal justice system in this country, federal, state, and local, receives less than 2 percent of all government revenues and less than three-quarters of 1 percent of our national income. We spend less on this pitifully inadequate system than we do on federal agricultural programs and little more than we do on the space program.

Responsibility for police, courts, and corrections has resided mostly with state and local governments. That is as it should be. But these governments do not have the financial resources to deepen their investment in improving the criminal justice system. The financial commitment must be a federal one. The federal government, after all, takes the lion's share of tax revenues; it ought to take the major financial responsibility for deterring crime, administering justice fairly, and bringing wrongdoers back into a productive role in society. The Council of Economic Advisers estimates that 19 billion dollars annually will be freed for domestic programs once our military engagement ends in Southeast Asia. A host of long-neglected needs at home will be competing for these dollars. The criminal justice system is only one of them. We ought to proceed now to plan the use of those future dollars wisely. A firm commitment now, in the form of the organic legislation, to increase greatly our expenditures on the criminal justice system would permit planners within the system to make effective reforms once the money becomes available.

I do not mean to suggest that the criminal justice system should be given priority over all the other competing needs of our society. Quite the contrary. In our report to the President, the National Commission on Violence spoke of the twin objectives of making violence "both unnecessary and unrewarding." Neither corrective approach will succeed without the other. Making violence unnecessary is nothing less than the task of giving all Americans a satisfactory stake in the life of the community.

We must seek to eradicate poverty where it persists, improve education where it is deficient, and provide health care in areas of the community where it is inadequate and beyond the financial reach of citizens. Efforts to remake our cities must include steps to eliminate the ghettos, to provide decent housing for everyone, to build effective systems of mass transit (especially for those who cannot afford automobiles), and to assure adequate measures for the upkeep of every neighborhood. Our national goal should be the dignity of work for every citizen capable of work. Our overriding goal, in all such programs, should be to provide every citizen a stake in the community. The citizen who has much to gain by living by the rules and in concert with his fellow citizens has much to lose by defying the rules and rebuking the community.

I add the caution that we ought not to pursue these social measures merely in the name of crime eradication. The high correlation of the outward symbols of deprivation—bad housing, low educational achievement, high unemployment—with violent crime does not mean that improvements in the former will lead inexorably to complete elimination of the latter. Physical conditions can be changed by concerted effort, but attitudes and habits will change only through inner enlightenment. The human animal is complex, and there is more to violent crime than a simple reaction to alienating circumstances. We ought rather to undertake these social reforms because they are the proper, humane things to do. Reordering our national priorities to give new emphasis to the quality of life for every citizen is a realistic goal for this affluent society. It is a worthy new phase for a nation that has subdued a continent physically and accomplished so much technologically.

These are matters not to be left to government alone. It is the job of all of us, as private citizens, to seek deep understanding of the problem of violence in our society, to voice concern over the deficiencies in our society that give rise to violence, and to help remedy these deficiencies. It is the job of local schools, churches, and citizens' groups to emphasize and transmit, more effectively than they have in the past, the values that will make our society more humane and less violent. It is also their job to lend encouragement to youth to participate creatively in the society. It is the job of our nation's scholars to seek a better understanding of the roots of violence and to design and evaluate more effective measures for discouraging it. And it is the job of all of us, but especially of those privileged by education, to repudiate violence and to live by the precepts of tolerance, reasonableness, and civility so that others may see that violence is unnecessary and, measured by the highest standard, truly unrewarding.

I conclude this overview of a troublesome national problem with two quotations from the report of the Violence Commission to the President. We said, "Order is indispensable to society, law is indispensable to order, and enforcement is indispensable to law." And then, to make the thought complete and legitimate, we added, "The justice and the decency of the law and its enforcement are not simply embellishments, but rather the indispensable condition of respect for law and civil peace in a free society."

THE HISTORY OF

AMERICAN VIOLENCE

henry steele commager

1

THE HISTORY OF AMERICAN
VIOLENCE: AN INTERPRETATION

Introduction: How symptomatic it is of our troubled
and uncertain times, our crisis of confidence of the
1970s, that Henry Steele Commager, a veritable dean of
American historians, should reassess our violent past in
the following essay with such powerful anger and condemnation. In *The American Mind*, the widely dis-

Henry Steele Commager taught American history at Columbia University from 1938 to 1956, and he has taught at
Amherst College since 1956. He has served as visiting professor at numerous other American universities and has also
held appointments at Cambridge, Oxford, the Royal University at Uppsala, the University of Copenhagen, and the University of Santiago, Chile. His voluminous publications include *The American Mind* (New Haven: Yale University
Press, 1950) and, with Samuel Eliot Morison, the popular
textbook *The Growth of the American Republic* (2 vols.;
New York: Oxford University Press, 1930, and five revised
editions).

cussed and celebrated interpretation of the modern American character which Professor Commager published in 1950, he affirmed in his conclusion that:

The American was still optimistic, still took for granted that his was the most favored of all countries, the happiest and most virtuous of all societies, and, though less sure of progress, was still confident that the best was yet to be. Two world wars had not induced in him either a sense of sin or that awareness of evil almost instinctive with most Old World peoples and had but accentuated his own assurance of power and success.

As for his politics and government, the American had proved himself "politically mature: he made the two-party system work, achieved reforms by evolution rather than by revolution, produced able leaders in times of crisis, and maintained liberty and republican institutions in times of war." Commager was not uncritical in 1950 of the twentieth-century American, his inherited attitudes, and his institutions. But contrast the optimistic assessment above to the shattering indictment of the historical performance of the American state below, which is drawn from the essay that follows:

The elementary fact which glares upon us from every chapter of our history and stares out at us from every page of our daily paper is that the major, the overwhelming, manifestations of violence in our history and society have been, and still are, official. In America violence is clad in the vestments of respectability and armored with the authority of the law. It customarily took and takes the form of assaults on the weak and the helpless, on the whole of society, on future generations. It is violence against the native peoples, Negroes, immigrants, women and children, perishing and dangerous classes. It is violence against nature herself.

We have come a long way since 1950—McCarthyism and the Korean War; the souring and splintering of the civil rights movement; the assassinations of our leaders; Watts and Kent State; Vietnam, My Lai. In light of our tumultuous present, our past must be freshly reinterpreted, and if the deep reservoir of American optimism and confidence is not exhausted it is sorely depleted. What can our past tell us about the origins of our current malaise and how best to respond to it? In the first section of the extensive essay below, Professor Commager first defines in very broad terms the persistent phenomenon of American violence and then describes its salient features. In the second section he seeks to explain its enduring pathology by examining the underside of five historical circumstances that in our historical literature have customarily been adduced to account for America's unique virtuosity. In the final section he rejects as inappropriate and self-defeating three contemporary "get tough" attacks on the symptoms of violence, and calls instead for a concerted and much-belated assault upon its underlying symptoms.

ALMOST ALL THE COMMENTARIES ON and studies of violence in America define violence narrowly and describe it in conventional terms. Violence is commonly, though not universally, equated with lawlessness; it is almost always physical in the ostentatious sense of inflicting bodily harm or physical damage at a particular moment. But violence, as we all know, is, or can be, something quite different from this. To strike a child is quite clearly to do him violence; what shall we call condemning him to work eight or ten hours daily in a textile mill? To lynch a Negro is clearly violence; what shall we call keeping him in slavery for a lifetime? To condemn a woman or a child to a rat-infested cell for no fault or crime is violence; so is condemning hundreds of thousands of women and children to rat-infested slums in Harlem or Watts for years at a time. Though the report of the National Commission on the Causes and Prevention of Violence devotes substantial space to the history of violence, it does not—perhaps could not—address itself to these and similar manifestations of violence: the effective destruction of the Indians, the exploitation of immigrants and of women and children in industry, and so forth.

So it has ever been; so it still is, in our consciousness. It is the Indian attacks on white settlements—King Philip's War or the Deerfield massacre—that get attention in the textbooks rather than the systematic destruction of the Indian by warfare, smallpox, whisky, or the starvation which followed the seizure of their lands and the killing of the buffalo. It is the slave uprisings, the Denmark Vesey affair, the Nat Turner "rebellion" that command attention rather than the savage reprisals against slaves for real or imagined injuries or the systematic violence inherent in slavery on almost every plantation over the long years. And so it is today. No one can examine the Walker Report on the riots in Chicago in midsummer 1968 without concluding that the police perpetrated more and more senseless violence against demonstrators and bystanders than the other way around; but public opinion and the courts blame the demonstrators. No one can study the recent Scranton Report on what is called the Kent State tragedy without realizing that it was the National Guard that was guilty of reckless and unjustifiable violence towards students, not the other way around; but the Portage County grand jury exonerated the guard and indicted the students.

It is sobering that this is habitual. Histories of violence rarely embrace such chapters of history as the genocide against the natives of Mexico and Peru, which reduced their population from perhaps 20 million to 3 or 4 million in half a century; or the slave trade which brought altogether some 4 million blacks from Africa to America, nine-tenths of them to Brazil and the Caribbean. They do not commonly include the story of child labor in the mines and the mills of old England or of New; the exploitation of women in factories or in domestic service; the denial of education to millions of children; the condemnation of immigrants to ghettos and slums of our great cities during much of the last century—the assaults by respectable society on what Theodore Parker called the perishing and dangerous classes.

We could do worse than to return to that magnificent sermon preached in 1864 by the man who earned the title "the great American preacher," Theodore Parker. Let me quote the opening lines:

There are two classes of men who are weak and little: one is little by nature, consisting of such as are born with feeble powers . . . the other is little by position, comprising men that are permanently poor and ignorant. When Jesus said, It is not God's will that one of these little ones should perish, I take it he included both these classes— men little by nature and men little by position. Furthermore, I take it he said what is true, that it is not God's will one of these little ones should perish. Now, a man may be said to perish when he is ruined, or even when he fails to attain the degree of manhood he might obtain. . . . In a society like ours . . . with such a history, a history of blood and violence, cunning and fraud; resting on such a basis—a basis of selfishness; a society wherein there is a preference of the mighty, and a postponement of the righteous, where power is worshipped and justice little honored, though much talked of, it comes to pass that a great many little ones from both these classes actually perish.[1]

Violence takes many forms. Our daily speech testifies to the variety of meanings we read into the word. Thus we speak of violating territory, violating a treaty, violating a promise, an oath, or a law. Literature is filled with references to the violence of party faction; philosophy rebukes those whose notions violate logic or truth. When we speak of violating the rights of man—once a favorite phrase of Americans—that term has reference to more than the use of deliberate force: it embraces habitual misconduct by government or society; it covers precisely such episodes as those at Jackson, Mississippi, or at Lamar, South Carolina, such conditions as those described by Oscar Lewis in his study of the Sanchez

---

[1] Parker, "A Sermon of the Perishing Classes in Boston.—Preached at the Melodeon, on Sunday, August 30, 1846," in *Speeches, Addresses, and Occasional Sermons* (Boston: Rufus Leighton, Jr., 1860), 1: 185–86.

family or by Claude Brown in his moving *Manchild in the Promised Land*.

The elementary fact which glares upon us from every chapter of our history and stares out at us from every page of our daily paper is that the major, the overwhelming, manifestations of violence in our history and society have been, and still are, official. In America violence is clad in the vestments of respectability and armored with the authority of the law. It customarily took and takes the form of assaults on the weak and the helpless, on the whole of society, on future generations. It is violence against the native peoples, Negroes, immigrants, women and children, perishing and dangerous classes; it is violence against nature herself.

Our inability or reluctance to recognize this is part of that deeply engrained confusion which E. A. Ross analyzed over sixty years ago in his classic *Sin and Society* (1907). The argument which Ross then advanced is still valid: that we are bemused by Old Testament concepts of sin—sin as personal, overt, and ostentatious—and that we satisfy our yearning to prove our virtue by punishing such sin, and sinners—the drunk, the wife beater, the embezzler, the thief—while we overlook the malefactors whose crimes are corporate, absentee, and impersonal. "Unlike the old-time villain," wrote Ross, "the latter day malefactor does not wear a slouch hat and a comforter, breathe forth curses and an odor of gin, go about his nefarious work with clenched teeth and an evil scowl. The modern high-powered dealer of woe wears immaculate linen, carries a silk hat and a lighted cigar, sins with calm countenance and a serene soul, leagues or months from the evil he causes. Upon his gentlemanly presence the eventual blood and tears do not obtrude themselves." It could be a description of our own contemporaries, those who produce cancer-causing cigarettes, lying advertisements, worthless cereals, worse than useless drugs, defective automobiles, airplanes that pollute the air, and chemicals that destroy life in the streams. Thus, Ross noted, failure to observe fire regulations, install safety devices in factories or railroads or automobiles, or inspect unseaworthy boats might take a fearful toll in lives, but none supposed those responsible guilty of murder. Thus improper inspection of banks or security exchanges, false statements in company prospectuses, and speculation in grain might bring poverty to thousands, but none of those involved thought themselves guilty of larceny. Business competition might force the employment of children of nine in the mines or dictate the use of women labor in sweatshops, but none of those involved thought themselves guilty of slavery. The purchase of votes, the corruption of election officials, the bribing of officeholders by holding out the promise of future rewards, and the flagrant defiance of the law might threaten the very foundations of democracy, but none of those involved in these shabby practices thought themselves guilty of treason.

This reasoning applies with equal relevance to the problem of violence. It is the destruction of a building by arson that outrages us, not the destruction of a forest of redwoods by a plywood company; it is the assault on individuals that disturbs rather than poisoning a generation with polluted air or cigarettes. It is the spectacle of campus demonstrations that brings calls for law and order—and brings the National Guard, too—rather than the systematic denial of constitutional rights to millions of Negroes over a century of time, and now.

Official violence characterized American policy toward the native races from the beginning of our history, in Virginia and the Bay Colony, and on a hundred frontiers from those of New England and the Carolinas to those of the farthest West. The story is too familiar for repetition. The greatest example of genocide in history, certainly up until the Nazi destruction of Jews, was that which Europe inflicted on the Indians. If the English killed off fewer Indians than did the Spaniards, that was because there were fewer to kill. They did a pretty thorough job and continued to do so long after there was even the faintest justification for murder and destruction as a form of defense. Thus the massacre of the Conestoga Indians by the Paxton Boys in 1764; the cruel Indian removals of the 1830s—official this time; the Black Hawk War, with its monstrous massacre of women and children of the Fox and the Winnebago; the Chivington massacre of 1864 (women and children again); the massacre of the Sioux, of the Nez Percé, and so on to the end, when the Indians were finally cooped up in reservations. Even today we take their lands from them.

In this first and most continuous display of violence we can see some of those features that were to persist and to characterize much of our history. First, the mixture of the private, the semiofficial, and the official, with everywhere a general public countenance of what was done. Second, the almost invariable application to violence of a patina of moral justification: it was all the will of God, for the Indians were heathens and probably children of Satan; it was manifest destiny, for Providence itself meant that America should expand from sea to sea; it was even legal, for an inferior people has no right permanently to deny access to the land by a majority of civilized people who need it. And from the beginning, too, it was justified by the application of that double standard which we still cherish and apply. The roots of the double standard —one for the civilized nations of Europe, the other for the backward nations of the rest of the globe—are, of course, in Old World philosophy, and this standard flourished for four hundred years, applied enthusiastically by the Spaniards in Peru, by the British in India, by slave traders in Africa, by most of Europe in China. It is rather out of date now, but we still cling to it in Vietnam.

The second pervasive and persistent manifestation of violence in America is also still with us: violence against nature. No other people in history, with the exception of the Arabs, have ravaged their natural resources so ruthlessly and so speedily as have Americans. The explanation is rooted in history. From the beginning Americans had "land enough for our descendants to the thousandth and thousandth generation" (the words are from Jefferson's first inaugural). They were bemused, that is, by the concept of infinity of resources of all kinds. The explanation is rooted, too, in our special kind of society—a society where men were not bound to the soil or the workbench but could strike out on their own; a society where there was, from the beginning, a premium on private enterprise and where those who opened up new lands, cut down forests, and dammed up streams were regarded as public benefactors; a society where men were or thought they were equal, where each man had, therefore, an equal right to the land and its resources, and each generation, too, an equal right with its fathers and forefathers. In that kind of society it was almost inevitable that each individual, each group, each corporation would exploit as much as it could as fast as it could.

The destruction of nature in America began early and has continued at an increasing tempo to our day. As early as the 1790s André Michaux complained that there were no real stands of timber left along the Atlantic coast from Maryland north, and as pioneers girdled the trees or burned them the forests retreated ever westward. It was not only the forests and the land that were ravaged. Soon the beaver, the buffalo, the fox, the carrier pigeon, even the eagle were threatened with something like extinction. In the single year 1854, Chittenden tells us, more than 400,000 buffalo were killed, for the most part wantonly.

The process continues unabated. Lake Erie is dead, Lake Michigan is dying, and a hundred smaller lakes like the once lovely Onondaga in upstate New York are chemical cesspools. Fish are driven from our rivers and our lakes; the shad no longer swim in the Pedee or perch in Erie; lobsters are dying off from DDT and Alaska seal from mercury poisoning, while the birds have all but disappeared from many parts of our country, leaving the countryside prey to insect invaders. By what authority have corporations indulged themselves in destroying the resources of the country but by the authority of power?

Can this process properly be called violence? Clearly we have violated the land and the flora and fauna on the land, which are not really ours to violate but belong to those generations whose future glory moved Jefferson to rapture. If this destruction were perpetrated by a single individual—if, let us say, a trustee destroyed a forest which was under his fiduciary protection or killed

off a herd of cattle which he was required to conserve—the violence and the criminality would be universally acknowledged.
What Americans have been doing for two centuries and what we
continue to do on an ever more audacious scale is to destroy the
inheritance of future generations. The fact that hundreds of millions of children are being deprived of their just inheritance mag-
nifies the crime a thousandfold.

The third large chapter of violence tells the tragic story of violence toward the Negro, for two centuries as slave, for another
hundred years as freedman. It is the ostentatious expressions of
violence that have always aroused our indignation—the violence
depicted by *Uncle Tom's Cabin* and a hundred other abolitionist
tracts; the violence of the some 5,000 lynchings in the South between 1882 and the end of the 1920s; the race riots, from those in
New Orleans and New York in the 1860s to those in East St.
Louis, Chicago, and Detroit in our time. But as Aristophanes said
2,500 years ago, "There are things, then, hotter than fire, there
are speeches more shameless still. . . ." If we assume that the only
violence against blacks was the violence of the whip, the branding
iron, and the faggot, we may congratulate ourselves that violence
against the blacks is a thing of the past. But the violence which
whites inflicted on blacks was a day-after-day affair, the violence
of imposing inferiority on fellow men, of denial of full manhood
and womanhood, of poverty and ignorance and social contempt.
Much of this persists, not in the South alone, as the Negroes themselves know, but in Harlem and Watts, in Philadelphia and Washington, in every industrial city of the country. This is a violence
that is rooted deep in the minds and hearts of the American people,
a violence that has been nourished by miseducation, pride, and
arrogance for two centuries. What we need today to temper our
indignation against the palpable fact of black violence in almost
every city of the country is something of that humility and insight
that animated Abraham Lincoln in his second inaugural address
when he prayed that the scourge of war might pass away. But

if God wills that it continue until all the wealth piled by the bonds-
man's two hundred and fifty years of unrequited toil shall be sunk,

and until every drop of blood drawn with the lash shall be paid by another drawn with the sword, as was said three thousand years ago, so still it must be said, "The judgments of the Lord are true and righteous altogether."

Slavery inflicted violence upon whites as well. To defend slavery the South violently silenced all critics. Preachers, editors, and teachers were driven out or driven underground. To oppose slavery, much of the North resorted to violence—the violence of the rescue of fugitive slaves from the hands of the slave catchers, the violence of the Christiania riot or the breaking into jails at Boston and Syracuse and Racine, Wisconsin. Representative Brooks's attack on Senator Sumner was the very symbol of the resort to violence, the confession that even in the halls of Congress reason was not to be relied upon, but force. Symbolic, too, were the hundred canes that southern admirers sent to Brooks to replace the one he had broken over Sumner's head.

Nor is it the Negro alone who has been the victim of official and unofficial, but generally accepted, violence. The Mexicans, the Puerto Ricans, the Orientals, even minority groups among immigrants—the Irish, the Italians—have suffered indignities and violence. The melancholy record is set forth in a hundred volumes from Jacob Riis's *How The Other Half Lives* to Oscar Lewis's *Children of Sanchez.* These are the poor and the weak, often the perishing classes. We received them, to be sure, the tired, the poor, the huddled masses yearning to breathe free, and gave them freedom from the worst of tyrannies and persecutions. Where we inflicted violence upon them it was not so much out of malevolence as out of thoughtlessness and ignorance. It was easier to exploit than to welcome, and the process of Americanization, as we are now coming to recognize, was long and arduous.

Fourth, violence against minorities is dramatized in the statistics of crime. But crime itself is often a form of class struggle: perhaps we should say that class struggle commonly takes the form of crime. When we note that the number of Negroes arrested and convicted of crime is widely disproportionate to their numbers, we cannot conclude that Negroes have some innate propensity to crime.

Rather we must conclude that crime is a form of protest against a ruling class that deprives the perishing classes of equal opportunities in work, education, and the benefits of society and imposes upon them ceaseless humiliations and degradations symbolized by the slum. We must conclude that the disproportionate numbers of arrests and convictions reflect, too, the double standard applied almost instinctively by police—one for those who are white, respectable, and prosperous; another for those who are not white, do not seem respectable, and are clearly not prosperous.

What is true of violence against the blacks is coming to be true of violence against the young. This is something new in American experience. In the past the young in America were pampered and exalted. Ours was a society where it was taken for granted, and quite rightly, too, that each new generation would be better, stronger, and cleverer than its predecessor. That mood has passed —temporarily, I trust—and has been supplanted by an ugly mood which looks upon the young with suspicion, malice, and envy and equates a college degree with a criminal record. The disproportionate number of criminals—or alleged criminals—among the young is not, as our Vice-President would have us suppose, an indication of some special perversity. It is perhaps an expression of a kind of class warfare waged with the most miscellaneous weapons, often those of violence, between the generations.

But it is not crime we are concerned with but violence. It is fairly clear, I think, that much of the crime of minority groups or the young is itself a product of violence; that the so-called criminals are often the victims of violence both before and after arrests; that in many cases it is society that has already perpetrated a kind of preliminary violence against them. This is sometimes true in a naked and unashamed fashion: thus the physical attack on a group of Black Panthers by the police in a Brooklyn court— an attack which has gone unpunished; thus the affair at Kent, Ohio, where the National Guard killed four young prople and the grand jury returned indictments not against the guardsmen but against the victims of their assault.

There is another element of the perishing and dangerous classes subject to ceaseless, massive, and direful violence: the victims of our prisons. Our prisons have been a scandal for over a century. Every year there is some revelation of fresh outrages and horrors —murders in Arkansas, sexual attacks in California, neglect and betrayal in New York. Compared with the prison systems in the Scandinavian countries, American prisons are barbarous. The Constitution prohibits cruel and unusual punishment. None familiar with the violations and humiliations daily inflicted on thousands of prisoners can doubt that these are the victims of cruel and unusual punishment.

The fifth broad area of violence in American history—never wholly official, but for the most part countenanced by public opinion—has been that directed against religious minorities. The Quakers in the colonial era were pressed to death, some of them were whipped out of town, were denied rights accorded to other people. In the nineteenth century Catholics were the objects of violence—witness the burning of the Ursuline Nunnery; and in the West, the Mormons.

More pervasive and persistent than religious violence has been industrial violence, a subject familiar to all of us. Here again it is fair to say that labor on the whole has been the victim of violence rather than the perpetrator and that most of the violence directed against it has come from authority—from the police, state troops, the National Guard, or officially recognized private police forces like the Pinkertons. But as with the history of slavery, it is not primarily in the story of the Ludlow Massacre, the war in the Colorado coal fields, and the violence at Homestead, Pullman, and Gastonia that we trace the impact of violence. It is rather in the violence done to "the least of these"—to the women and children working in factories and mills and to the families living in wretched company houses on credit grudgingly extended by the companies. It is in the denial, until states tardily got around to dealing with the matter, of compensation for industrial accidents, which were more numerous than in any other industrial country. It is in the long hours of labor; as late as the 1920s steelworkers worked a twelve-hour day and a seven-day week, and hours in the textile industry averaged from sixty to eighty-four a week, even for the women and children who constituted a large part of the labor force. If an individual treated a twelve-year-old child as corporations treated their child labor even in this century, we would call the police. The fact that the abuse of children in factories and mines was not generally recognized as violence by those who were responsible for it is no more persuasive than the fact that slaveowners generally insisted that slavery was a positive blessing.

Finally there is the violence of war. War is always and everywhere violent, and it cannot be argued that Americans have been more guilty here than others. But it can be said that some of the wars in which the United States has been engaged were unnecessary and therefore inexcusable. And it can be said that there was less excuse for Americans to resort to war than for most peoples, for we were from the beginning a nation dedicated to isolation from the wars of the Old World, to the subordination of the military to the civilian, and to the search for peace.

Certainly our Indian wars were, for the most part, unnecessary and were conducted with an excess of violence and of barbarism. The Mexican War, it is now generally conceded, was an unnecessary war, carried far beyond its original bounds and purposes. The Phillippine War, which Americans have for the most part conveniently forgotten, was all but inexcusable and was attended by the use of concentration camps, torture of prisoners, and barbarism much like that which has attended our war in Vietnam.

What is the explanation of this long and sobering record? The search for causation in history is vain, for every event has a thousand antecedents, most of them hidden from the prying eye of the historian. We are able, however, to distinguish some aspects of our experience that illuminate the American propensity toward violence. We are, all of us, creatures and even prisoners of the past;

even those who rebel against the past confess thereby their dependence upon it. As Emerson put it in his essay on "The Conservative": "The past has baked your loaf."

First, then, in the words of Lewis Mumford, the settlement of America was the unsettlement of Europe. First, that is, the uprooting and transplanting, the rapture of the existing fabric of society, the breaking of the cake of custom. Think what it meant to pull up roots and travel thousands of miles to a strange land, to break violently with family and neighbor, with familiar ways of farming and of labor, with the all-encompassing church, with the network of friends, with the protection of tradition, with the security of language, and come to a strange new world. It might almost be said that every emigrant had, at the outset, a traumatic experience with violence—that moving to America was in a psychological sense an act of violence. Nor was this something that ended once and for all with the founding of America. It was a process repeated generation after generation among those who migrated and repeated decade after decade by those already in the New World for every move to a new frontier: from Boston to the Connecticut valley, from the valley to Vermont, from Vermont to upstate New York, from New York to the Ohio country, from Ohio to the Dakotas or to California.

Second, inextricably connected with this first, was the absence of most of those institutions which were the foundation and the framework of society and which had given form and meaning to life. In Europe there was the church, the guilds, the class society, the family network, all with their assurance of obligation and security. Once in the New World men were on their own, divorced, often enough, even from family, divorced from obligations to the guild, or the feudal overlord or the landlord, from the priest or the parson. "Take but degree away, untune that string, and hark, what chaos follows," wrote Shakespeare, and what he said was to some extent applicable to the New World, where there were no degrees in the Old World sense of the term.

We must not exaggerate. From the beginnings Americans made

heroic efforts to recreate an orderly society in the New World, to erect barriers against the wilderness, savagery, and barbarism. They built churches, set up schools, established (certainly in New England) trim little communities, instituted governments and enforced laws, and they created orderly and law-abiding societies. But none of this could stand against the lure of the wilderness or prevent the violence of Indian warfare or of the disruption of family and community ties or of the ravaging of the soil. It is fashionable to blame much of American violence on the frontier and to conjure up, in defense of that argument, the history of frontier lawlessness and vigilantism. All true enough, no doubt, though frontiers did not always act this way. But what the frontier contributed to violence was not in these occasional and dramatic displays of lawlessness so dear to the imagination of the film and television mongers, but the deeper and more pervasive violence of isolation—the kind of thing described so movingly in that great novel of the frontier, Ole Rolvaag's *Giants in the Earth*, or suggested in these lines from *John Brown's Body*, by Stephen Vincent Benét:

> I took my wife out of a pretty house.
> I took my wife out of a pleasant place.
> I stripped my wife of comfortable things.
> I drove my wife to wander with the wind.

A third consideration illuminating the habit of violence in America is the special nature of American idealism and the concept of American uniqueness. I have in mind that deeply rooted notion of New World innocence and Old World depravity to which I have already referred; that great theme which runs like a scarlet thread through so much of American history from the Jeffersonian rejection of Europe to modern isolationism, from Crèvecoeur's celebration of American virtue and innocence to the more profound and subtle exploration of that theme by Henry James. The myth of natural superiority and the myth of uniqueness joined to form and sustain that double standard which has for so long been one of the most striking features of American conduct and morality. As we were a special people creating in the New World a new Zion, we were not to be judged by the standards by which we judged other nations. What was imperialism in other nations was manifest destiny in America. What was a class society elsewhere was here but the normal operation of the economy and of private enterprise. Our political system was unique—and indeed it was: it was free of corruption and of privilege. When corruption and privilege came, as they inexorably did, this could all be charged against immigrants who did not understand America, those who spoke with "accents of menace alien to our air,/voices that once the tower of Babel knew . . ." who had somehow passed through the "Unguarded Gates." Other nations waged wars of conquest, but our wars were just. As William Vaughan Moody put it in that great poem of protest, "An Ode in Time of Hesitation":

> . . . The wars we wage
> Are noble, and our battles still are won
> By justice for us, ere we lift the gage . . .
> The proud republic hath not stooped to cheat
> And scramble in the market-place of war. . . .

I do not need to make explicit what is implicit in all this. Other nations should submit their disputes to international tribunals, as we once did. But that no longer applies to us, not in any event the disputes in the Caribbean, not the disputes in Southeast Asia. Other nations should forgo the dangers of nuclear weapons, and when China detonated her first weapon President Eisenhower said that it was a dark day for humanity. We are so far the only nation that has ever used the nuclear weapon in war and we have the largest of all nuclear stockpiles, but this is not relevant, for there is no danger that we would ever misuse our power. Germany and Japan are bound by rules laid down or formulated by the Nuremberg Tribunal and the Japan War Crimes Commission, but these do not apply to us. We are the most humanitarian of nations; our humanitarianism can be taken for granted. We need not sign the international agreements on the use of chemicals and gases that bind other nations, nor need we sign the convention for human rights. In other areas, too, the double standard is taken for granted. We felt no such indignation when our marines invaded Santo Domingo in order to control an election there as we did when the Russians invaded Czechoslovakia for much the same purpose. China is not a "peace-loving nation" and is therefore justly excluded from the United Nations. But we, though our nuclear bases all but ring both China and Russia, though our giant navies command the Mediterranean and the China seas, and though we spend more on the military than any other nation, are by definition "peace-loving."

It is pointless to elaborate on anything so familiar, but it is relevant to emphasize the relationship of these myths to the problem of violence. What they do is, in a sense, sublimate violence, give to it a curious kind of moral quality.

Fourth, another of our original virtues was exploitation for purposes of aggrandizement, and the exploitation was often attended by violence. I refer to the principle of equality of opportunity and the celebration of enterprise. From the beginning America put a premium on individual enterprise and held out the promise of limitless rewards to those who displayed it. It promised the millenium without producing it. Private gain was identified with public. Those who conquered the soil, built railroads, and set up factories were public benefactors, no matter how they did it. Law was expected to accommodate itself to progress, and from the beginning there was a premium on certain kinds of lawlessness. The DAR, which deplores lawlessness among the young, does not, I believe, deplore the lawlessness of the Boston Tea Party, or the evasions of the customs regulations which Parliament imposed on Americans, or even the malpractices of pioneers who squatted on royal or proprietary lands, or the dissenters who flouted the requirements of religious conformity and the authority of the established church. What was true for the early chapter of our history remained true for the later: for lumber companies that invaded national forests, for cattle companies that built fences around public land, for mining companies that took minerals and oil where they could find them. Indeed, we make heroes of them now and even celebrate in a hundred westerns their violence against Indians, settlers, and nature.

It was inevitable that in a new country there should be a premium on aggressiveness. So there was in the Spanish dominions in America, although their government and church established their authority and imposed their own kind of law. But America had a different inheritance and a different philosophy. It was, at the beginning, the philosophy which Tom Paine summed up in an epigram: "Government, like dress, is the badge of lost innocence." Government was by its very nature dangerous and should be kept to a minimum. But where government was weak and was expected to be weak—where, indeed, it was often looked upon as the enemy to freedom—there was an irresistible temptation for society to take the law into its own hands. The vigilante tradition in America—what Tocqueville early identified as the tyranny of the majority—is not a manifestation of American depravity but an almost inevitable product of the philosophy that that government is best which governs least. By a striking but not surprising paradox, this principle flourished along with the counterprinciple that the majority has a right to impose its will on minorities and dissenters and nonconformists, for the voice of the people is indeed the voice of God. This partially explains (the explanation is, of course, more complex) the persistence of the American habit of people's taking the law into their own hands—the vigilante tradition of the West, now pretty generally admired by Americans; the lynchings in the South; the acceptance by large elements of our population of the antics of the Ku Klux Klan; the tolerance for the lawless use of governmental power (I do not call it authority) by an A. Mitchell Palmer after World War I or by the McCarthyites after World War II or by Attorney-General John Mitchell in our own day. The English do not take the law into their own hands because they have confidence in the ability of their police and their courts to enforce the laws.

The breakdown of law today is, as the presidential commission has made clear but as is not clear to presidents, not a satanic up-surge of wickedness, unprecedented in our history, but a·symptom of the loss of a sense of community. It has its roots in the soil of majoritarianism, in the distrust of government, even in the principle and the ideal of equalitarianism. Its virulent manifestations to-day are a symptom of and an expression of the weakening of that sense of community which has hitherto held together our vastly heterogeneous society. Government cannot be expected to enforce community standards, especially if there is no longer any certainty about what are community standards. Where tradition and com-munity opinion break down—and they break down in part because the public is too bewildered to have clear and reasoned opinions—men everywhere resort to force. Those who oppose a war think it quite proper to evade the draft by any means or in extreme cases to fall back on dynamite, just as extremist labor groups, excluded from the economic consensus, fell back on dynamite in the nineties and the early years of this century. Where the law seems unable to deal with dissent or nonconformity—even such mild nonconformity as is expressed in the life styles of the young, in long hair and hippie clothes and violent language—the public reacts violently. What is most sobering about Kent State is not the hysterical reaction of the National Guard but the considered reaction of the grand jury that asserted the necessity of shooting in the face of youthful misconduct and the reaction of the public, which endorse those findings.

Finally, most important of all as an explanation of the present crisis of violence is the power of the example of government. It is a commonplace that in a democratic society government reflects the moral standards of the people. It is not perhaps sufficiently appre-ciated that in such a society the moral standards of a people will tend to reflect those of the government as well. Resort of our gov-ernment to violence is nothing new. Witness the prolonged violence against the Indians as an expression of official policy, the violent ousting of Mexicans from their territories, the violence of the Philip-pine War, the violence of Vera Cruz or the Bay of Pigs or Santo

Domingo. But never before has violence on a massive scale been so deliberately adopted by government as now, when we are all so fearful of violence. Never before has it been so stubbornly maintained, so defiantly justified. Never before has what it is popular to call "overkill" been so triumphantly elevated to official policy—the overkill of dropping nine times the tonnage of bombs on Vietnam that we dropped in the Pacific War, the violence of deliberately selecting civilian rather than military targets and inflicting more casualties on civilians than on the military, the violence of concentration camps, the violence against nature herself in the chemical warfare and the defoliation program. What the American people are required to witness now—quite literally, on television—is not the ordinary violence of war. It is the extralegal violence repudiated by Americans in World War II (at least when practiced by the enemy) and punished in the Nuremberg and the Japanese war trials. These practices are not defended on grounds of necessity, for not only is there no necessity for this kind of warfare, there is no necessity for the war itself. They are justified rather on the ground that it would be shameful for the United States to lose a war in which it was engaged or on ideological grounds wholly alien to American experience.

Of what use is it for the President to authorize and perpetrate this violence in his capacity as commander-in-chief and then to deplore violence on the campus or in radical demonstrations in his capacity as President? Americans, like all people, believe what they see, not what they hear. Because they have a long tradition of freedom in access to all information they are perhaps more prone than other people to this. What they see are government leaders who ceaselessly intone the litany of law and order while resorting to insensate violence, who justify that violence on grounds that can only be designated irrational, and who impatiently brush aside conclusive evidence that the violence it practices was held criminal by the courts we ourselves set up just a quarter-century ago and that the war we fight and the quasi-wars we conduct are generally regarded as violations of international law.

The conclusion seems inescapable to me that violence in the United States will not abate until we have abandoned and repudiated the kind of violence we ourselves practice in Asia. Violence, like order, is a seamless web. It is not feasible to indulge lawlessness and violence in one realm of society and government and to decry it in others. It is absurd to suppose that we can restore respect for law and order to our society when we display to it and the world contempt for law and for order in foreign policy. Nor can we expect to solve those problems which glare so hideously upon us while we dissipate our resources, moral and intellectual as well as economic, in senseless overseas ventures. It was said centuries ago of slavery that those who would enslave others must first enslave themselves. So we can say that those who visit wanton violence and destruction on others will find violence and destruction at home.

If this analysis is correct, it suggests:

First, the futility of most of the current attacks on violence by those who simplify the problem by reducing it to one of permissiveness, of the breakdown of moral standards, of the natural depravity of the young. Well might we say as we contemplate the ravaging of nature, the gross injustices of our social and economic establishment, and the conduct of the war in Indochina, "Look who is talking about discipline."

Second, the futility of tougher laws, tougher cops, tougher National Guards, and tougher judges as a remedy for anything; or, on a somewhat more sophisticated level, the futility of the reversal of Miranda and the reinterpretation of due process by the Supreme Court. For this approach does not even pretend to get at the causes of violence in the United States. Rather it promises more violence and more lawlessness.

Third, the futility of moral admonitions, of clarion cries for discipline, of finding scapegoats—Dr. Benjamin Spock, for example (as unlikely a scapegoat as ever lived), or college professors collectively. There is no faintest likelihood that the problems that confront us will fold up and go away because we invoke a new and more alliterative rhetoric.

There is no ultimate solution to the problem of violence, for propensity to violence is deeply embedded if not in human nature then in Western nature. But it would be a counsel of despair to conclude that there are no ways to mitigate our current crisis. We can at least try to shift our fascinated gaze from the mere manifestations of violence to its underlying causes. We can at least try to deal with those forces which appear to account for violence.

First, we should insist on real equality, political and legal, for the Negro. If he was assured of this he could, I think, be trusted to achieve economic opportunity and social equality in time. Certainly with equal access to the polls and to office and with the assurance of equal protection of the laws, something he does not now enjoy, he will be removed from the category of those whom the majority, or its officials, can savage with impunity.

Second, we should seek to recover the sense of fiduciary obligation to posterity that animated the generation of the founding fathers and write it into law. We should, that is, make it impossible for private individuals or corporations, or our own governmental agencies like the Corps of Engineers or the Atomic Energy Commission, to continue the pollution and destruction of our natural resources. This is not the place to draw up a program for the reestablishment of the fiduciary principle, but you will permit me one elementary observation, based I believe upon a reading of our history: that governmental regulatory commissions are almost routinely captured by the interests they are supposed to regulate and will not do the job; that mere financial penalties will not do the job any more than they have done the job with, say, the traffic or the parking problem or the oil pollution problem; that only criminal penalties will, in the long run, be effective.

Third, we should abandon our current military malpractices and return to the traditional principle and practice of the subordination of the military to civil authority and, what is really more to the point, the subordination of military to civilian interests. We should cease providing our own people, and the world, the spectacle of massive violations of distant countries, violations of neutrality by our CIA, violations of international law, and violations of the United Nations Charter, and restore that respect for the supremacy of the law that characterized us through most of our history.

Fourth, we should abandon the double standard of morality for private and for public conduct, for individuals and for corporations, and for national and for international policies that makes a mockery of our declamations against domestic violence and of our pretensions to moral leadership in the world.

"The care to preserve society," wrote Grotius, "is the source of all law." It is the function and the purpose of all law as well. We use power and even law today to fragment society. We do this on the domestic arena. We do it even more violently throughout the globe. We cannot preserve even our own society unless we commit ourselves to the preservation of society everywhere. Hunger and disease are not national but global, and so too the violence that they spread. Pollution is not national but global, we cannot pollute our own waters or skies without polluting the waters and skies that belong to all mankind. Science and education are global—even, as we have learned, in the marginal manifestation of unrest in the universities; we cannot divorce ourselves from the great community of learning or openly flout the famous dictum of Edward Jenner: "the sciences are never at war."

What Jefferson admonished us in his first inaugural address, that we should "restore that harmony and affection without which liberty and even life itself are but dreary things," should be our guiding principle on the world as on the domestic stage.

II

CRIMINAL VIOLENCE AND

AMERICA'S PUBLIC INSTITUTIONS

earl warren

2

THE COURTS

Introduction: Former Chief Justice Warren's guarded acknowledgment in the essay that follows that the Warren Court's efforts "to reconcile law enforcement methods with constitutional safeguards . . . created controversy" represents both discretion and an understatement of monumental dimensions. For under his leadership from 1953 to his retirement in 1969 the Supreme Court accomplished what has been acknowledged by both friends and opponents as a veritable "revolution in due process" in criminal law.

The Warren Court inherited a complicated legacy in

A native of California, Earl Warren served as district attorney of Alameda County from 1925 to 1939; as attorney general of California, 1939–43; and as governor of California, 1943–53. In 1948 he was the Republican candidate for Vice-President, and in 1953 he was appointed Chief Justice of the U.S. Supreme Court by President Dwight D. Eisenhower, a post from which he retired in 1969.

criminal law, but the historic thrust of precedent had been to confine judicial scrutiny of the rights of the accused to the relatively rare federal criminal offenses and to allow state courts, where the vast majority of criminal cases were tried, wide discretion in determining just what the defendants' rights were—or, more often, were not. The reasoning here was that whereas citizens' guarantees under the Bill of Rights were clearly protected from federal violation by the Fifth Amendment's due process clause, the Fourteenth Amendment of 1868 did *not* automatically extend those rights to protect the accused against state infringement. Well before Earl Warren became Chief Justice in 1953, the Supreme Court had begun the slow, piecemeal process of extending Bills of Rights guarantees to defendants in state criminal prosecutions by linking these rights to the accused through the Fourteenth Amendment's due process clause. But the liberal Warren Court vastly accelerated this process of federal accretion and reversal of precedent, and in the bargain it troubled some sympathetic students of the law and enraged hardline law-and-order conservatives who pointed alarmingly to soaring crime rates and then accusingly at the Warren Court.

Symbolic of the Warren Court's alleged "coddling of criminals" and "handcuffing of police" was the ruling of 1966 in *Miranda* v. *Arizona*. It held that the police before interrogation must advise a suspect that anything he says may be used against him and that he has the right to remain silent, to obtain a lawyer of his choice, and to have a lawyer appointed if he is indigent. The controversy over this ruling became so heated that the Congress in Title II of the Omnibus Crime Control and Safe Streets Act of 1968 came perilously close to withdrawing the court's jurisdiction to review such state criminal rulings. The act did explicitly seek to blunt the impact of *Miranda*, *Mallory* v. *U.S.* (which in 1957 ruled as excessive delay a ten-hour police interrogation after arrest and prior to arraignment), and *U.S.* v. *Wade* (which in 1967 guaranteed suspects a lawyer at police lineups).

That, in brief, is the background of the storm over the Supreme Court and rising crime. The court has yet to review the Omnibus Crime Act of 1968, and, ironically, most independent authorities have concluded that the Warren Court's sympathetic rulings have made very little dent in state criminal convictions—most of which, in light of today's jammed dockets, are secured through plea bargaining anyway. Former Attorney General Nicholas DeB. Katzenbach estimated that the Warren Court's rulings probably affected less than 1 per cent of all criminal offenses. But if the Warren Court got what was largely a bum rap for spurring rising crime— demographic trends, drugs, and the general social pathology of the exploited ghetto are far more to blame, as Milton Eisenhower explains in his Introduction and Overview—the issues of increasingly clogged courts and their appalling delays, and the scandalous distortion of priorities which is reflected in the miserly budgets of the federal and state judiciaries, are compelling causes for concern and even alarm. Earl Warren discusses these pressing issues below, together with his intriguing and "firm belief that organized crime can never exist in any large community unless one or more of the law enforcement agencies have been corrupted."

FOR YEARS WE HAVE BEEN STUDYING CRIME, its causes and it cures. In 1965, President Johnson appointed a Commission on Crime in the District of Columbia. After many months of diligent labor it issued a report that stimulated a few days of news coverage, after which it came to rest in the National Archives. In 1965 he also appointed a Commission on Law Enforcement and the Administration of Justice. After a few years it also reported and, with a like amount of news coverage, quietly took its place alongside the earlier one in the archives.

In 1966 the same President appointed the National Commission on Reform of Federal Criminal Laws. It has not yet reported but has worked diligently since that time and is expected to report in the near future.

In 1967 President Johnson appointed the National Advisory Commission on Civil Disorders. Its findings were reported in what is known as the Kerner Report, named for its chairman, the then governor of Illinois and now a judge of the United States Court of Appeals for the Seventh Circuit. That followed the fate of the others.

In 1968 President Johnson appointed the National Commission on the Causes and Prevention of Violence and named as its chairman the distinguished president emeritus of The Johns Hopkins University, Dr. Milton S. Eisenhower. After approximately eighteen months of arduous labor and with the help of a large number of natural and social scientists and knowledgeable public-spirited officials and laymen, a thoughtful, well-balanced report was issued pointing out the causes and remedies for our perilous condition. It, too, inspired a few days of notoriety and now rests with the others in the same status of "innocuous desuetude." I say this not in derogation of but in admiration and appreciation of the contribution made by Dr. Eisenhower and his commission. They rendered a great service to the nation and, like the others that preceded them, their findings are entitled to more objective treatment than has been accorded them.

Even more recently, in June 1970, President Nixon appointed the President's Commission on Campus Unrest with William W. Scranton former governor of Pennsylvania, as chairman. That commission, with as difficult an assignment as one could undertake in these days and with great fidelity, reported on September 26, 1970. Although it was roundly castigated in high places for some of its findings, it has not yet been officially recognized.

In addition to these commissions, there has been a Civil Rights Commission since March 1958 investigating conditions which have been responsible for much of the crime we have today. It has done a noble job and has reported annually, but in spite of its great importance and its objectivity it has received little official recognition.

All of these presidential commissions, composed of able conscientious citizens functioning in a bipartisan manner, have given their best efforts to be objective and have not differed greatly in their findings. Yet most of their work—indeed, the most fundamental parts of it—has been ignored. As a result, crime has increased and violence is a greater problem for the nation than it was before the first of the commissions was appointed.

It is particularly pertinent to reflect upon this part of recent history because the people of the United States, rightly alarmed about the amount of crime that exists today, are anxious for the answers to our dilemma of being the most affluent country in the world and, at the same time, subject to the most violence because of poverty, ignorance, and degradation. At this particular time they are grievously disappointed.

We recently went through a great national campaign in which the major issue was "law and order." For months in every state of the Union we heard the issue raised in strident terms, but with no discussion of the causes or proposed cures for criminal conduct. It consisted of accusations by one group of candidates against the other, the main one that of being "soft on crime." Those accused were so busy defending themselves against the accusations and so fearful of being further accused that they suggested no basic remedies. As a result, the entire campaign was one of harsh rhetoric and a search for scapegoats responsible for the situation. Some blamed the courts; some blamed the police; others blamed the members of Congress for inaction. And the campaign ended with the people in utter confusion.

It was only in very rare instances that any of the candidates running for office or the institutions of government could be said to be in favor of or even "soft" on crime. If we are to really do anything of importance in stemming the tide of crime and violence, it is time for all of us who are engaged in making the law or in interpreting it or administering it to stop looking for scapegoats and to recognize that all of us have a heavy responsibility to do our own part and an obligation to do it in cooperation with the others rather than in conflict with them.

In doing so, we could well remember the biblical admonition, "And why beholdest thou the mote that is in thy brother's eye, but considereth not the beam that is in thine own eye?" No branch of the government today is working to its full potential to eliminate violence and crime, and no one of them at its greatest potential is capable of accomplishing the hydra-headed job alone.

Most of the crimes which come to our immediate attention and which most often arouse our emotions of fear and insecurity—the so-called crime in the streets—are murder, rape, robbery, burglary, major thefts, and the like. Most of these occur in our cities and particularly in our major cities. They are spawned in the ghettos which are to be found in most of our large urban areas. These are the centers where the poor, the disadvantaged, the uneducated, and the unskilled gather and live in degradation because there is no other place for them to live. Shorn of pride and self-respect and victimized by sharpsters of all kinds, many of them lost their respect for law and the methods of its enforcement.

It has been pointed out so many times by the commissions which have studied the problem and by others who are familiar with urban life that so long as this abject poverty, ignorance, and degradation prevail we can look for very little, if any, improvement in the situation. It is recognized by thoughtful people that the elimination of these slums has been neglected for many years because we have been lulled into inaction by the cliché that we cannot afford both guns and butter at the same time. For the past thirty years the vast preponderance of our money and resources has been spent on foreign wars—hot, cold, or both.

During all that period, while our great advances in science and technology and particularly automation have lured our dispossessed poor from rural areas to the slums of the cities in their effort to share the benefits of what we have proudly proclaimed as the most affluent society in recorded history, we have been unable, or at least unwilling, to find the money to help the cities carry their backbreaking burden. As a result they have become cancerous and metastatic, and the disease is spreading over the entire nation. I do not pose as an expert on our crime problem, but I do feel certain it is our greatest domestic problem, that we are not solving it, and that it is growing in intensity.

It has been a long time since I was intimately connected with community problems and seventeen years since I have been associated even with state government. In that length of time, one necessarily becomes dated so far as the details of such a many-sided problem are concerned. But there was a time—for twenty years, to be exact—when every waking hour of my time was devoted to the enforcement of the law and to improving the administration of justice. In retrospect, people today are inclined to believe that the problems are different now and that the breakdowns in the administration of justice are something new to present-day society. But I can say to you, with full confidence, that the conditions we face today are not unlike, except in degree, those confronting us in my days in law enforcement work in California from 1920 to 1940.

As evidence of that fact, I would refer you to the reports of the presidential commissions appointed to investigate crime by President Hoover in 1930 and by President Johnson in 1965—the Wickersham report of the earlier year and the report of the President's Commission on Law Enforcement and Administration of Justice in 1967. They are different not in content but only in time and persons involved.

It was my lot to serve as a district attorney in Alameda County, a coastal and industrial community of 600,000 people, during the rum-running, hijacking, bootlegging, and organized crime of the prohibition era. This was a time when, in a number of the largest cities of the country, a man could not engage in honest business without paying tribute to organized criminals. It was to prevent this and the accompanying murders from becoming a way of life in California that I spent twenty years of my life in law enforcement. And I can say to you without embarrassment that we—the district attorneys, sheriffs, and police chiefs of California—successfully organized to prevent this from becoming a reality in many of our cities. It was not easy to do, but we operated on the theory that if these professional racketeers who tried to come to our state from other parts of the country were thwarted before they were big enough to have political power, it was not an impossible job.

I am not saying, of course, that we did not have our share of bootleggers and rum-runners. We did, largely because the people did not consider it to be unworthy to deal with them for the liquor they desired. As almost any adult of those days can recall, that in itself caused corruption among law enforcement agencies in many California communities. But the other rackets were reduced to a minimum.

Since those years I have not been entirely removed from such problems because I spent eleven of them in the state capital of California and then sixteen on the Supreme Court of the United States. As governor I was deeply concerned with developing conditions, and through the instrumentality of a crime commission and in conjunction with law enforcement agencies I kept abreast of and, in some instances, ahead of those who endeavored to corrupt the state. In the later years on the court, of course, we came into contact with many phases of the crime problem, and under conditions which caused us to reconcile law enforcement methods with constitutional safeguards.

This has in itself created controversy because of the interpretation of constitutional provisions which sometimes appear to conflict with each other. There is no way of satisfying both of the contending forces. Courts cannot, no more than would Solomon, divide the baby between two women who claim to be the mother of the child. They must constantly bear in mind the admonition of Benjamin Franklin that "those, who would give up essential liberty to purchase a little temporary safety, deserve neither liberty nor safety."

I must be frank and state that I have not done any recent research in criminology nor studied carefully all of the reports of the various commissions and committees which have recently investigated crime. But throughout a half-century I have formed certain opinions concerning the administration of justice, and these I am willing to share for whatever they may be worth. I start from the premise that there is no American problem entitled to higher priority than that of making safer our homes, our places of business, and our streets.

There are, as we all know in broad general terms, two kinds of crime: organized crime and individual crime. In dealing with the organized crime it is my firm belief that it can never exist to any marked degree in any large community unless one or more of the law enforcement agencies has been corrupted. This is a harsh statement, but I know that close scrutiny of conditions wherever such crime exists will show that it is protected. The business rackets which were so prevalent in other days and which, to some degree, still exist could not have permeated a great city without the corruption of some of those who were charged with the enforcement of the law. And we are told by the crime commission of one of our largest cities that between 1919 and 1966 a thousand gangster murders were committed there and that only twenty-three persons have been convicted for the killings. That result bespeaks a connection somewhere between law enforcement and organized crime.

The narcotics traffic today, which is destroying the equilibrium of our society, could never have become as pervasive and as open as it is unless there was connivance between authorities and criminals. For years we have watched this traffic develop from a stage which now seems to us to have been small to one which threatens our entire future because it has become a subculture oriented toward our young people. However, let me hasten to say that it is not the young people who are manufacturing these narcotics; it is not the young people who are distributing them nationwide; and it is not the young people who are making untold millions of dollars in the traffic. The young people are the victims as well as society of this breakdown of law.

And with all of this taking place, practically all we see by way of law enforcement is the arrest of an unfortunate user, a neighborhood "pusher" who in all probability is himself a user, and the occasional confiscation of a cache of narcotics which is infinitesimal in the context of the traffic, but without any really important arrests. This is nothing new in principle but only in degree. We can never make a dent in the narcotics traffic until we can ferret out and sequester those who are at the top of this horrible crime against society and also those who are protecting it.

Practically all the states in the Union have stringent laws against gambling. Yet we are told that illicit gambling amounts to 20 billion dollars a year and that the profits add up to 7 billion dollars. This is one of the greatest strongholds of organized crime in the nation, and still we are told by the law enforcement agencies in many cities that it is almost impossible for them to locate and bring to justice anyone except a few in small betting establishments or those selling lottery tickets on the streets.

About ten years ago a high law enforcement official in the District of Columbia testified before a congressional committee that the numbers racket alone amounted to 500 million dollars annually in the district, which is only about eight miles square, and yet it was impossible to find out who was running it or how to put a stop to it. The loan shark business in some of our cities has become an inhuman affair to the extent that necessitous borrowers who are unable to pay the exorbitant interest charge against them are beaten and even maimed for life by the loan shark, both as punishment for failure to pay and as a lesson to others. This practice thrives in many cities; yet we seldom bring the perpetrators to justice. We find these same practices brought close to legitimate business through extortion, blackmail, and other criminal activities. Many other kinds of crime could be accounted for in like manner.

Then there is the problem of individual crime. So bad has it become in some places that it is no longer safe for a woman to go to the stores to do her shopping even in the daytime. The crimes committed at night against innocent people are appalling. This, too, has become one of the most serious problems of American life.

For such criminal conduct there are a myriad of reasons, and the time available would not permit a thorough discussion of it. But we do know that many of the social conditions which prevail in the nation today contribute largely to it. We know that the conditions in many of our cities' ghettos, where the poor, the uneducated, the unhealthy, and the underprivileged are congregated, are the sources of much of this crime. It should be pointed out that most of the crime stemming from the ghettos is imposed on the families who are forced to live there. It is a big subject which involves psychiatry, psychology, and sociology, in none of which I am qualified to speak. But as laymen we must know that we cannot have a healthy city if we have a cancerous ghetto; nor can we have a healthy state if we have a sick city, any more than we can have a healthy body if we have a diseased organ of any kind.

Having worked with law enforcement officers for as many years as I did, I have a great sympathy for all of them—the police, the prosecutors, and the judges. The conditions which I have described cannot be attributed in the main to any one of the three. They all have their strengths because they are principally manned by honest persons with good motivations. They likewise all have their weaknesses, however, and I propose to point out what I consider to be the greatest weakness of the judicial process because it is the judiciary to which I have latterly been giving my greatest attention.

In my opinion, the greatest weakness of our judicial system is that it has become clogged and does not function in a fluent fashion to determine promptly the guilt or innocence of those charged with crime. In many communities it takes from three to four years to have a jury trial in a civil case, and in many of those same jurisdictions it will take a year or more to have a jury trial in a criminal case.

Addressing myself to the criminal side only, I had occasion

about three years ago to study the criminal calendar in the United States District Court for the Eastern District of New York in Brooklyn. I knew they were having difficulties; but I found, to my dismay, that the average time between indictment and jury trial was 22.2 months. Add to that the time between arrest and indictment and you will find that it was approximately two years from the date of arrest until the date of the jury trial. That cannot result in justice. If an innocent man is required to wait two years for a jury trial, even if he is acquitted he has lost those two years of his life by reason of the cloud which has been hanging over him. On the other hand, if a man is guilty and has been out on bail for two years between the time of his arrest and his conviction there is no way of knowing how many crimes he may have committed in the meantime. Under no circumstances can that be justice to the people of the community.

Now just what causes this delay and what can be done about it? Most judges, like most other people in public life, are honest men and women. Most of them are diligent in their work. Yet their calendars become congested in some such degree. There are a number of reasons for this, the principal one being that the judicial process and the judicial machinery and procedures were never designed to carry the load of litigation that they are now called upon to handle.

Let us just view the situation since around the first of the century. At that time there was no automobiles. Today there are 101 million. There are 105 million licensed drivers, and almost everyone in the nation rides in these cars and with these drivers. In 1968 55,000 people were killed on our highways and 2 million were injured in automobile accidents. The litigation generated by these deaths and injuries now constitutes a major portion of our judicial work and slows all other litigation down to a slow walk.

Since the turn of the century many phases of the law have developed which now generate complex and necessarily lengthy litigation—antitrust law, labor law, tax law, regulation of public utilities, and a score of other fields which could be mentioned. Cases in these areas and the normal litigation which flows from the more complex relationships of individual to individual and individual to the government in a nation of 200 million people have brought our courts to the point of frustration and near paralysis.

In the meantime, our judicial system has not grown as have the other branches of the government. Recall, if you please, how small the executive branch of the government was in 1900 and how pervasive it is now. Imagine how small the legislative establishment was at that time and how enormous it is today. But the courts have not grown with any such rapidity, although the demands on the courts have been in keeping with the expansion of our population and our economic and political life.

I sat on the Supreme Court of the United States for sixteen years, and during that time the personnel on the court increased by only eleven persons, all of whom were stenographic, clerical, or housekeeping employees. This is only a fraction of the increase in staff personnel of any one congressman or senator during the same period. Still, all the requests by the courts for additional help were denied. The other courts of the nation are in much the same situation.

The Supreme Court has been able to keep its calendar current, but only because it has the right to determine what cases coming before it are appropriate for argument. The courts of appeals and the district courts, however, must hear every case that comes to them, and the time necessarily consumed is getting far beyond their control. They must have additional and more experienced clerical personnel, researchers, and administrators to relieve the judges of details so that they may apply themselves to the process of judging cases.

One of the most important phases of judicial work is to have adequate research. We now have in the judicial systems of the states and in the federal courts more than 3 million reported decisions. Happily they are indexed with proper citations, but research is time consuming, and a judge cannot sit on the bench all day and then do the necessary research to meet the problems of his cases.

I could go on, but the fact is that the size of the judiciary, the machinery for its operation, and the personnel to support it must be brought into keeping with the conditions of the last third of the twentieth century instead of those of former days. If this is done I am sure the courts will respond in kind and give the people of the United States that standard of justice which is their due, and that this improvement will do much to contain crime within bounds.

I must admit that the courts through the centuries have been very conservative institutions, apprehensive of change and functioning in isolation. It has not been easy to convince many judges of the necessity for accepting modern methods of procedure and administration. Now I believe that all but a very few are convinced that if courts are to be able to serve their true purpose they must be adjusted to current conditions and that they must be relieved of administrative details so they may devote their full time and energy to the judging process.

This suggestion is not one which would disturb the national fiscal situation. It cost 328 million dollars to build our last modern cruiser for the Navy. In 1969, it cost 128 million to operate our whole federal judicial system. This is six-hundredths of 1 percent of our national budget—a small amount, indeed, to spend toward the internal security of our nation.

Finally, I must say that in searching for means to reduce crime the full responsibility should not be put upon any one or all of the law enforcement agencies. The police, the prosecutors, the lawyers, and the courts have great burdens to carry in this field, but they cannot be justly charged with all the conditions that bring crime to such gigantic proportions. They are not responsible for the ignorance, the poverty, the disease, the degradation, or the racial tensions which exist in the ghettos, nor for the millions of drunks and alcoholics who contribute so much to crime. Certainly they cannot be faulted for the debasement of the stage and screen nor for the appetite of the public for the pornography and sadism which is so pervasive in both forms of entertainment.

Neither can they be held responsible for the aura of violence which has been fed by war through the past quarter of a century. They cannot be accountable for the failure of citizens to report crime or to give testimony concerning it.

These are things that society in general has responsibility for. We hear much these days about the necessity for cooling off the economy to stop inflation. It is about time that we take steps to cool off society if the law enforcement officers of the nation are to be expected to stop the inflation of crime. Much of our problem lies in the areas of poverty, housing, education, health, race discrimination, and inadequate training and facilities for law enforcement officers. If we will but commit ourselves as a nation to these problems, as we have committed ourselves to recent wars and to flights to the moon, we can cool society and win the war against crime and violence.

gerald r. ford

3

THE CONGRESS

Introduction: On January 4, 1965, Republicans in the
House of Representatives voted 73 to 67 in a secret
caucus to replace Charles Halleck with Gerald Ford as
House minority leader. While Representative Ford cannot claim to speak for the entire Congress—no single
member can, of course—he does largely represent the
consensus of House Republicans, and in the 1968 vote
on the Omnibus Crime Control and Safe Streets Act,
which constitutes the most extensive anticrime legislation in the nation's history, Mr. Ford's views generally

Gerald R. Ford has been representative to Congress from
Michigan's Fifth Congressional District since 1948; in 1965
he was elected House minority leader by his Republican col-
leagues. In 1961 the American Political Science Association
conferred on him its Distinguished Congressional Service
Award. He was appointed to the Warren Commission by
President Johnson in November of 1963. A graduate of the
Yale Law School, he is a veteran of World War II.

prevailed over those of the lame duck Johnson administration, which had originally proposed the bill.

Congressional liberals and civil libertarians had generally objected to the bill's provisions for block grants to the states, rather than directly to local communities, to assist in law enforcement; to its broad wiretapping authority; to its direct attack upon the Warren Court's solicitude for the rights of the accused; and to substantially weaker firearms controls than those the administration had originally requested. But the conservative majority prevailed, and President Johnson reluctantly declined to veto the bill, which the *Congressional Quarterly* called "a major defeat for the Administration and Congressional liberals."

In the discussion below, Congressman Ford reflects the hardening national attitude toward criminal violence, whether it occurs on the manifestly unsafe streets, is plotted in the councils of the "syndicate families," or is spawned on the nation's campuses. He acknowledges that "many sociologists tell us that the roots of crime can be found in the basic conditions of life." But he concentrates his fire on leftist subversion, on the politicians' inflated promises to the poor, and on the general disrespect for law occasioned by the civil rights protests of the 1960s, wherein moral objections to particular laws allegedly sanctioned their wholesale violation. These are, of course, debatable assertions, as Professors Frankel and Zinn aptly demonstrate in chapter 10. Furthermore, Ford's description of campus disorders, which is based upon unspecified FBI sources, pictures a rather monolithic view of unprovoked assaults upon constituted authorities by a conspiratorial array of SDS, Weathermen, Black Panthers, and the like, who have "connections" with Arab terrorists and the Communist regime in North Vietnam. One need not deny the partial truth of this to insist that there is more to campus strife than radical conspiracy. But, appallingly, the hard evidence does lend strong support to Ford's third contention: that in light of the Eisenhower Commission's estimate that at best only half of all serious crimes are even reported, that just 12 percent lead to arrest, that only 6 percent of those arrested are convicted, and that only 1½ percent are imprisoned "is it any wonder that the criminal today believes that crime *does* pay?"

IN CONSIDERING WHAT I WOULD SAY HERE, I at first thought of concentrating all of my discussion on campus disorders. But after further reflection I decided to cover almost the entire range of violence on the American scene today—and this of course includes all types of violent crime. I will, then, discuss not only campus disturbances which erupt into violence but also street crime and organized crime. Let me turn first to campus violence.

The colleges of America are in crisis. They are not caught up in crisis because of peaceful dissent. They are torn by disruption and the politics of confrontation—the politics of violence. But there can be no sensible remedy for the problem of campus violence without the maintaining of a sense of perspective. By that I mean that we first of all must recognize that less than 200 of our institutions of higher learning have been ripped by violence while some 400 others have suffered through some form of nonviolent disruption. There are, in fact, nearly 2,600 colleges and universities in America with a total enrollment of more than 7 million students. The vast majority of these students neither takes part in nor sympathizes with campus violence.

But we must be deeply concerned with the campus violence that does occur, since it not only tramples on the rights of nonviolent students but also results in property damage and occasionally even the loss of life. We are all familiar with the confrontation politics of the campus—nonnegotiable demands, strikes and boycotts, arson, willful destruction of property, assault and battery, the occupation of buildings, interruption of classes, disruption of meetings, the barring of entrances to buildings, holding administrators captive. On a few campuses it seems clear that revolutionaries seek nothing less than the destruction of the university.

To those who are quick to condemn college administrators, let me say that no university can avoid a confrontation with those who are determined to engage in revolutionary politics. *The actions of the militants on our campuses are completely without justification.* If they have legitimate grievances, they have a right to present those grievances, individually or collectively. They have a right to ask that those grievances be given a respectful hearing and that appropriate remedial measures be adopted. But they have no right to interfere with the proper functioning of any university or college. They have no right to prevent other students from pursuing their studies. They have no right to destroy property or occupy school buildings by sit-ins or sleep-ins. For any student violation of civil or criminal law there should be *no amnesty.* There should be appropriate punishment, fairly adjudicated and administered but inexorable.

The universities themselves have the primary responsibility for maintaining order on campus. Properly so. However, in cases where they are unable or unwilling to perform the function, outside intervention becomes not only necessary but mandatory. Where outside intervention becomes necessary, the essential ingredient for control of the situation is planning. Plans must be formulated between the university and civil authorities to deal with campus violence if it should occur. I understand this was not true at Kent State University. Yet at no time should a university administration completely abdicate its role to the civil authorities. We *can* maintain order on our campuses—and I speak only of doing so in a manner that does not interfere with the right of peaceful dissent. We must ensure freedom of dissent while preserving order. These two goals are not incompatible. In fact, they should be inseparable.

Students should be allowed freedom of dissent as long as they do not interfere with the rights of others. That is the key to campus discipline and an orderly pursuit of learning. Students should be dealt with firmly if they engage in willful defamation, public obscenity, incitements to crime, and any other civil or criminal misconduct. Today's generation of college students is perhaps the most idealistic in the history of America. This speaks well for the future of this country. But that idealism should express itself in pressure for peaceful change—for changes within the system. Does any American in his right mind really believe that the quality of life in this country would be improved by tearing down our system of government and destroying our large corporations? Has Marxism eliminated the evils of this earth?

In the 1969–70 academic year there were 1,800 campus demonstrations. The FBI reports that these demonstrations resulted in 8 deaths, 462 injuries, and 7,500 arrests. Two-thirds of those injured were police officers attempting to control the demonstrations. According to the FBI, militants engaged in 247 instances of arson, 313 sit-ins in academic buildings, and 282 attacks on campus ROTC facilities. Property damage was estimated at 9.5 million dollars. In a recent bombing case, that at the University of Wisconsin on August 22, 1970, one student was killed and three others were injured.

During the last academic year the SDS and black militants were responsible for a sharp increase in racial disorders on campuses and in nearby areas. The number of these disorders increased by 68 percent over the previous year for a total of 530. Major racial disorders involving the SDS, black militants, and others occurred in 200 cities in 33 states and the District of Columbia during the academic year 1969–70. These disorders resulted in injuries to 500 persons, including 70 police officers and 30 teachers. Authorities made 1,800 arrests.

Two extremist groups, the Weathermen and the Black Panthers, are responsible for some of the most dramatic episodes of violence in this country. The Weathermen, an SDS splinter group, bombed a New York City Police Department facility and injured eight persons. The Black Panthers have committed 200 separate incidents of serious violence. Members of the Black Panther Party have been convicted in more than 400 criminal violations ranging from possession of explosives to murder. According to the FBI, the Black Panthers are directly responsible for killing 9 policemen and wounding 48.

The Black Panther Party has connections with the Communist regime in North Vietnam and Arab terrorists in Algeria and Jordan. Angela Davis, an avowed Communist with Black Panther connections, is alleged to be responsible for the murder of a state judge sitting in Marin County, California. She allegedly bought the guns in the killing. She is now in custody, under indictment for murder and kidnapping.

There is a comparatively new terrorist organization known as the East Coast Conspiracy To Save Lives. Its members include Father Philip Berrigan, who was apprehended by the FBI. This group talks of blowing up underground conduits and steam pipes in the District of Columbia and kidnaping high government officials. Their demands include an end to all bombing operations in Southeast Asia and the release of so-called political prisoners like the Black Panthers.

Yet as we read and talk of these terrorist organizations, and because they are so attention-arresting, we lost sight of the bulk of violence in the United States. We tend to forget that during the five-year period 1963–68, for instance, individual acts of violent crime resulted in more than 1 million injuries and over 50,000 homicides. We are inclined, too, to dismiss a rise in the rate of violent crimes by attributing it to an increase in the population. But the facts are that over the past decade there have been ominous increases in what we call the true rates of homicide, robbery, and aggravated assault. The true rates of these violent crimes now are the highest they have been since early in the 1900s. We lead the modern nations of the world in violent crime. Within just the past ten years the number of violent crimes committed in the United States annually per 100,000 persons has doubled.

The American public should not have to live in fear. Yet personal safety is at the top of today's public concern because the soaring crime rate has provoked fear and distrust in all Americans.

Many sociologists tell us that the roots of crime can be found in the basic conditions of life. If this is so, millions of Americans are asking themselves, why should America be plagued with a record-high incidence of crime in a time of affluence? I think the answer is many-faceted. First of all, many events of the sixties combined to cultivate a disrespect for the law. The feeling grew that if you disagreed with a law or a rule on moral grounds you were perfectly justified in breaking it. Initially this disobedience was passive, then it exploded into violence. Another reason for the sharp rise in crime, I feel, traces to the fact that the disadvantaged were promised much and received little. The third is that law enforcement has simply broken down in America.

We must, then, build on the wreckage of the sixties. We must rekindle respect for the law. We must make law enforcement processes work so that punishment for the guilty is swift and sure. In terms of social programs, we must not promise more than we can deliver.

We are, I believe, on the way to doing exactly what I have outlined here. We are more than doubling federal aid to local communities for law enforcement and court improvements under the Safe Streets Act of 1968. We have enacted legislation—the Organized Crime Control Act of 1970—which puts together an organized assault on organized crime and bombings in this country. We have launched the most progressive and far-reaching federal attack on drug abuse ever undertaken by the United States. And we have expanded our efforts in education and manpower training with a view to maximizing those efforts and delivering at least as much as we promise.

Long before the Organized Crime Control Act was approved, the administration began making life miserable for racketeers. The syndicate became an empire in trouble. To the gangster, the law suddenly became very menacing. The administration's beefed-up strike forces worked closely with state investigatory commissions to put the heat on the racketeers. The results are a testimonial to the administration's deep commitment to the war against crime. Of the six syndicate "families" in the New York–New Jersey metropolitan area, the leaders of five are either in prison or under heavy attack.

Now the weapons in the war against crime have grown in number and effectiveness through enactment of the administration's Organized Crime Control Act of 1970. Basically, the law provides for new perjury and contempt procedures calculated to induce reluctant witnesses to testify. It also provides stiffer jail terms for habitual criminals.

Besides giving authorities more weapons in the fight against crime, the new Organized Crime Control Act zeroes in on bombings, arson, and other criminal acts which have threatened to turn our citadels of learning into citadels of violence. The new law limits interstate traffic in explosives to licensees and official permittees and prohibits the sale of explosives to minors, felons, fugitives from justice, drug addicts, and mental defectives. It also brings the FBI into all bombing and arson cases at colleges receiving any form of federal aid.

Some Americans find it difficult to understand how a war against organized crime is going to help in fighting street crime. What they do not understand is that organized crime spawns street crime. Organized crime encourages street crime by inducing narcotics addicts to mug and rob. Organized crime encourages housebreaking and burglary by making it easy to dispose of stolen goods. Organized crime flourishes because of its virtual monopoly on illegal gambling, the numbers racket, and the importation of narcotics. An estimated 50 to 75 percent of the crimes committed on our nation's streets are perpetrated by drug addicts. This is why the administration is moving so forcefully to halt the importation of illegal narcotics.

We must, of course, attack crime on many fronts. That is why the aid we give to local police departments and our courts through the Safe Streets Act is just as important as our expanded effort against organized crime. As I mentioned earlier, our system of criminal justice has broken down and our deterrent to crime has therefore broken down with it. The National Commission on the Causes and Prevention of Violence—the Eisenhower Commission —has established that only 50 percent of serious crimes are actually reported, that just 12 percent lead to arrest, that only 6 percent are convicted, and that only 1½ percent are imprisoned. Is it any wonder that the criminal today believes that crimes *does* pay?

The following Eisenhower Commission statement should be imprinted on the mind of every American citizen: "The sad fact is that our criminal justice system, as presently operated, does not deter, does not detect, does not convict and does not correct." This is a serious indictment of American society. It is not only a charge but a challenge. And it is a challenge to which we must respond, a challenge we must meet. This is why I place such stress on the Safe Streets Act and the matching grants we are making under the program to strengthen our local police and overhaul our entire system of criminal justice.

Our system of criminal justice must be made to function efficiently. This is the only way to curb crime in this country. We must reach a point where the potential lawbreaker fears violating the law as much as innocent citizens today fear to exercise their right to move about freely in their communities.

The task of fighting crime is not hopeless; the battle is not in vain. We must persist in the fight against crime, and the American people must join the Congress and all of our state and local law enforcement agencies in combatting it. All of our law-abiding citizens must become concerned. They must become involved. There is no escaping responsibility in the war against crime. We *are* all involved.

I am cautiously optimistic as I look down the road. I see daylight ahead. The President is strongly committed to the control of crime. Washington is providing dollar help and other much-needed tools as well.

There is a commitment to the war against crime at all levels of government—federal, state, and local. And there is greater support each day on the part of all of our law-abiding citizens. What we must do now is to convince the criminal element in America that there is "no hiding place down there" and that punishment for their crimes against society will be swift and certain. I say we can do that. I say we are on our way. I say, let's get on with the job.

herbert g. klein

4

THE PRESIDENCY

Introduction: Since no president or serious presidential aspirant is going to be *for* violence, the tactical question in government and campaigning becomes how most effectively to oppose it. Republican presidents and hopefuls tend to call most stridently for no-nonsense police crackdowns to protect innocent citizens, and Democrats typically emphasize the need for governmental alleviation of the social ills that spawn criminality. Both tendencies are, of course, correct to a degree. In campaigning for the presidency in 1968, Richard Nixon ran on a platform which starkly warned that "lawlessness is crumbling the foundations of Ameri-

Herbert Klein is director of communications for the executive branch of the U.S. government. A native of California, he began as a newspaper reporter in 1940 and by 1959 had become editor of the *San Diego Union*. He has worked in public relations in support of Mr. Nixon's political campaigns since 1952.

can society." But party platforms are universally ignored both by the voters and the winners, and on the hustings in 1968 Mr. Nixon consistently avoided taking specific stands on key issues. The result was a campaign that was calm, efficient, dignified, and utterly boring—with the notable exception of Governor Spiro Agnew, who at one point charged that Vice-President Humphrey had been "soft on inflation, soft on Communism, and soft on law and order over the years" (a remark he was forced by embarrassed Republican congressional leaders to retract). But in appealing to the "forgotten Americans" who were the "nonshouters, the nondemonstrators," Mr. Nixon did accuse Mr. Humphrey of being "tragically naïve . . . about the nature of the crime crisis that grips America."

It is too early to determine whether Richard Nixon as President will be able to reverse the crime wave or end the war in Vietnam. It is clear that by 1971 the massive violence in the ghettos and demonstrations on the campuses had faded dramatically, although neither the ghetto nor the war conditions that prompted these protests had changed very much. Historically the federal government has had relatively little to do with criminal law enforcement, although federal and especially presidential policy and leadership has had a great deal to do with the social conditions that culminated in exploding ghettos and antiwar demonstrations. Perhaps it is fitting that a Republican president should largely ignore the report of the Scranton Commission on campus unrest, and ignore as well if not implicitly reject the recommendation of the President's Task Force on Low Income Housing that the trapped ghetto dweller be given access to the suburbs. In 1970 Mr. Nixon enraged open housing advocates and reassured many white home-owners when he pledged that "I can assure that it is not the policy of this government to use the power of the federal government or federal funds in any other way, in ways not required by the law, for forced integration of the suburbs." Yet his Democratic predecessor had largely ignored the Kerner Commission report, which had implied that the rhetorically inflated programs of the Great Society and especially the "war on poverty" had made little headway against the seemingly intractable social cancer that the ghetto represented and symbolized. Pundits chided President Johnson that in the war on poverty, poverty had won—that the antipoverty war's economic benefits had accrued largely to the growing army of highly paid consultants.

So perhaps American presidents, who head and symbolize our government, have been expected to accomplish too much both at home and abroad—at least as we have known them. Perhaps John F. Kennedy's moving inaugural address of 1961 ultimately invited the dour frustration of unrealistic hopes and unrequited dreams when he pledged: "Let every nation know, whether it wishes us well or ill, that we shall pay any price, bear any burden, meet any hardship, support any friend, oppose any foe to assure the survival and the success of liberty." President Nixon's domestic goals were at least more modest, if less noble. But despite his pledge and admonition to "lower our voices," the congressional elections of 1970 drew Mr. Agnew once again into the rhetorical limelight, this time with his primary target the press and the broadcasters. The Vice-President's virulent attacks prompted both fear and derision, but irrespective of his obvious partisan interests and of his charges that the media were dominated editorially by the viewpoint of the eastern liberal establishment, he had indirectly raised a very hard question, one which

Mr. Klein addresses in the essay that follows. That question is, does the media's commitment to report the news objectively play unwittingly into the hands of irresponsible elements who would manufacture "news" in order to secure free publicity for their views? This is a sensitive question on the political left these days, but in the early 1950s Republican Senator Joseph McCarthy shrewdly if irresponsibly developed the same technique of commanding headlines by continually making (and changing) charges of Communist subversion so rapidly that the media, which "objectively" reported his bizarre string of accusations, could never keep up —thereby largely forfeiting its important editorial role as interpreter and explainer as well as reporter of events. Mr. Klein's assertion that it would "not be totally accurate . . . to say that America is a violent society" does not altogether square with his subsequent allusion to our era of "actual revolution in this country today," but perhaps this reflects the conservative's customary tendency to defend the national legacy while deploring its detractors. On the whole, presidential press secretaries and directors of communications are not known for the vigorously controversial cutting edge of their remarks, and Mr. Klein's discussion is as true to this tradition as it is to the consistently conservative stance of the *San Diego Union* which he so long has served, and to the predominantly conservative stance of his President as well.

As DIRECTOR OF communications for the executive branch, and as a veteran member of the working press as well, I propose broadly to discuss the problem of violence in its relationship both to the presidency and to the mass media. Today we hear a great deal of public questioning about the balance of power among the various branches of government and among the major institutions of American society in general. Certainly there is a great deal of power resident in the presidency in our system, although executive power has historically been counterbalanced by the power of Congress and the judiciary. And certainly great power reposes in the media today, and it is growing in strength both in broadcasting and in the press. Finally, and above all, there is the power of the individual voter, the ultimate sovereign.

A president can recommend what laws we should have—especially in the area of maintaining public order, which bears most closely on the problem of violence—and he has then to turn to the Justice Department for the enforcement of those laws. But I believe that the most important contribution that a president can make lies in the less formal area of persuasion—the quiet adjustment of problems that might lead to greater violence if not handled properly. And a very good example of this has been the recent effort in the southern states to develop committees to look for problem spots and to implement effectively the most major program of school desegregation that has been attempted over the past ten years—one that thus far has gone very smoothly despite the great difficulties we have encountered in all these areas.

Regarding the power of the presidency, consider the analysis of one of our leading scholars in this area, the late Dr. Clinton Rossiter:

The role of the President that has undergone the most rapid growth in the past quarter-century is that of Protector of the Peace. Thanks to the eagerness with which Roosevelt and Truman responded to calls for help from the people, we now think of the President as a one-man riot squad ready to rush anywhere in the country to restore peace and order.[1]

While state and local authorities usually deal with fire, drought, pestilence, and violence, disasters that spread over several states

---

[1] Clinton Rossiter, *The American Presidency* (New York: Harcourt, Brace & Co., 1956), p. 90.

or touch upon federal interests are simply too hot for local authorities to handle unless they are certain of attention and action from the White House. And this, I believe, is one of the major problems: the American people expect too much of the president today. They look to him for powers that should no longer reside in his office—powers which I believe should be more locally allocated in the interest of getting the government back closer to the people.

So when you survey the powers of the presidency today, you find the authority to direct military policy, of course, and to provide leadership to the executive bureaucracy to a point, and to represent the country abroad and formulate foreign and domestic policy, and to provide moral leadership, as in the case of easing the transition to school desegregation in the South. But to cite Professor Rossiter again, any major reductions now in these powers of the President would tend to leave us naked to our enemies, to the invisible forces of boom and bust at home, and to the visible unrest and aggression abroad. In a country over which industrialization has swept in great waves, and in a world wherein active diplomacy is the minimum price of survival, it is less power than a vacuum of power that men must fear. So while I am convinced that we need to look for as many local solutions to our problems as possible, certainly I am not depreciating the need for a strong presidency, the type of strong, active presidency that has evolved over a period of time, basically from the days of Franklin Roosevelt.

It would not be totally accurate, I think, to say that America today is a violent society. It is not unfair to say, however, that America from time to time and place to place has been endangered by the irresponsible acts of a violent few. That violence exists in our society is patent, but we must keep its dimensions in perspective. We know that the perpetrators of violence respect no boundaries and no titles. Acts of violence have been directed at the citizens of our nation in the streets of its cities as well as at the President of the United States. Beyond the violence of individual criminal acts, we have seen the growth of invidious violence toward American institutions. If we did not know before, we must know by now that bombings, for example, do not destroy only property; they destroy people. Fires do not just burn establishments in buildings; they also terrorize society, disrupt cities, and wreak havoc on American society's attempt to conduct its own business in an atmosphere free from fear. Violence in the centers of our cities too often has plagued mostly the underprivileged, those who need the protection of society more than almost anyone else.

As for the relationship of the media to violence, surely the reader knows that members of the Nixon administration have not been hesitant in their criticisms of the media. And I think it is fair to say in a free and open society that members of the executive branch should not fear to voice concern over the media as long as the concern is never translated into coercion—which, by the way, has never been our aim in the administration and which is something the President and I are very strongly opposed to. However, while continuing to believe fully in the concept of free expression, it is clear to me that the media, including their educational and professional organizations, have shown an appalling lack of concern about the effects of particular media practices; they have shown insufficient interest in the internal search to determine how and under which reasonable standards they might do better. This rather categorical conclusion is certainly open to question, but it is a rather serious allegation that cannot totally be ignored.

First there is room, I think, for a positive acknowledgment of progress. Many newspapers have established new guidelines for the coverage of violence or civil disturbances, and this has largely been a development of the last five years. Network television has also made strides by investing in research to find out what effect their programs have on violence within our society. And certainly there have been many hearings in Congress which have developed additional information in this field. It is my hope that self-examination by the industry itself will not slow down but will accelerate so that we may find some answers to these most difficult questions. Second, and on the other side, there is still room for great improvement in the media's coverage of all news events. Is the coverage fair? Is it reliable? Do you depend upon it? What effect might the portrayal of violence have on the potentially violent? When criminal acts receive the attention of the press, is there an effect which encourages similar impulses on the part of other individuals? It is my belief that these are questions which must be answered in the 1970s.

Too often, I think, we look at violence as something which has just occurred in the last year or two. Yet in my home state of California we first had major riots on the campus of Berkeley in 1964. And I think one of the things to consider seriously is the danger that television and newspaper coverage of these events sometimes builds an obscure person into a national personality, a person with far more power than he has the right to have. Going back to 1964, there was the sudden projection of Mario Savio as a major spokesman for a lot who were violent on the campus. More recently we've seen demonstrations and violence on behalf of Bobby Seale. I wonder whether those who have been advocating support for Angela Davis on the campus of UCLA, who projected her into a major figure before she became involved in the possible implications of murder in northern California, examined in detail her credentials to be a spokesman for any one group. What were her credentials to be a national spokesman, someone who made headlines and captured major segments of the broadcast media? The question beyond what the individual thought and advocated is, how do the media themselves examine the projection of such figures? And beyond those figures who become nationally known because of violence, what are the media doing to cover those who don't participate in riots, those who make a conscious decision that they will seek a more moderate means of achieving their goals, the goals of progress for themselves, for their families and for their country?

I believe that certainly there remains the necessity for the media to continue to cover violence wherever it may occur. The question is whether reporting the action which takes place makes it necessary to also report the views in detail of each individual who suddenly projects himself or herself into national prominence and leadership because of that very coverage. Certainly I would not be in favor of suppressing the views of any individual or group, but I think there is little doubt that the media themselves have built these figures to a prominence that is denied those who have not earned their way to the top in this fashion. I speak of voices on campus, or in the street, voices of responsible leaders in their fields, who have developed very distinguished records and who have yet to utter their very first word on national television or have their names on page one of any newspaper in the country today.

What are the causes and effects of violence in relation to the media? Going back to the early days of the civil rights demonstrations, which in many ways were precursors to our modern disturbances, we can see that they certainly achieved a major constructive purpose because they called national attention to a problem which was being overlooked by the basic elements of society. And the progress which we have made in civil rights, progress which we must continue to pursue, has to be credited in large part to those who sacrificed and made what were designed to be peaceful efforts to call attention to the school problems in the South and other areas. But in the interest of looking at the causes and effects, too often, even in those early days, demonstrators who were seeking personal aggrandizement often waited until the cameras arrived, until the television turned on its light, until reporters appeared on the scene, rather than carry out the protest in a way which would logically and reasonably reach the conclusions they sought.

As an editor, I can remember in those earlier days the calls to my own city desk saying that if we failed to have a camera at a certain corner to cover the picketing of a bank, at an hour that they specified, then they would come down and picket the newspaper plant itself. I think this is the kind of thing which too often the media have bowed down to and as a result have in some way perpetuated violence by their failure to exert their own responsibility. This has been the subject of many major debates in meetings of American editors and broadcasters which I have attended. And I think, as I said earlier, that the result has been a more careful examination of the problem, which I believe needs additional study to pinpoint the relationships between causes and effects. It is a basic human trait, when someone turns on the televison camera, for everybody to wave so somebody at home will see them on the screen. And yet the very presence of the camera at some of the demonstration sites, I think, has certainly encouraged violence because of the fact that once it is there, the action is there, and in many cases when the cameras have failed to appear, violence has not occurred. I would have to say beyond that, however, that the intensity of any acts of violence cannot be directly attributed to the media. I think perhaps the start can be traced in many ways to the arrival of the camera, but certainly not how far this is carried, what the results are, what happens when the police and the protesters engage in a confrontation itself.

It is of major importance that we as responsible citizens together with the media, examine this entire problem today, because certainly it would be a major mistake if we went off the other end and said that we have to cut off all coverage. Banning news coverage would be the worst effect we could have in terms of perpetuating a free press, a press essential to a free nation. And yet the problem is becoming more and more complex as you look at the type of confrontation this country faces today. It is my belief that we are past many of the kinds of continual and massive confrontations between major groups, whether they be in the central urban areas or on the college campuses. And yet during 1970 we witnessed a growing amount of activity on the part of anarchists and revolutionaries, those who have chosen the route of hijackings and bombings. Those who, like the Weathermen, having planted the bomb, have now stepped forward to take credit for the fact that they, not someone else, were responsible for that act of violence. When you look at the growing era of confrontation this way, one of actual revolution in this country today, I think it is necessary not only to look at what we can do in terms of law to confront this, but also to ask whether it is a responsible action to show the videotape of the Weathermen as they claim credit for this violence. Is it responsible to broadcast their message in a way which can only lead to greater glorification of those who are dedicated to the overthrow of the free institutions of this country?

In looking at this from the viewpoint of government, there is no question that we need new tools. Many of these tools were supplied after long delay by the Congress just prior to the election of 1970, so we now have new laws for getting at organized crime and the problems of narcotics and drug abuse. We certainly have new laws which can provide federal help in investigating bombings in any building which is connected in any way with some type of a federal contract. One of the most interesting problems which now exists and is being funded generously, is the Law Enforcement Assistance Administration, which is operating under the Justice Department. In 1970 this program was funded at 63 million dollars, in 1971 at 268 million, and in 1972 at 480 million dollars for scientific study of, in part, the problem of the media in their relationship to violence.

In Buffalo these researchers have found, for example, that in one area where the crime rate was highest, the crime peaked on a given day at a given hour of each month. So there is, of course, one simple answer, which is to provide more police in the area during these recurrent periods of maximum crime. But the more complicated question is why this pattern—is it the reflection of the moon, or is it because something occurs involving paychecks on that day? I think that it would be safe to say that within the next two years crime will decrease in this country, largely because of the determination of the Nixon administration and largely because of the new tools provided for more law enforcement officers for greater means of getting at the problems themselves.

We hear a lot of comment today about government repression.

And certainly repression has been a serious concern of anyone in the United States since the earliest days of this republic. And yet, I think that the word is overused; it is a word which is used to describe almost any act that someone disapproves of. We have, for example, added a thousand police to the police force in the District of Columbia, and what we have found is that in doing this, while some have shouted repression because of things like no-knock legislation, the fact is that the crime rate in the District dropped down 25.4 percent between September 1969 and September 1970. I have made almost a lifetime of study of press freedom itself, and I count myself as one of those who speaks most forcibly in its behalf. Yet I hear also that we are trying to repress the press, that there is an effort to censor it. I find that there is no action taken by this administration which in any way either censors or represses the press. I believe the bigger danger today, really in terms of law itself, is in the acts of the Congress, which is reacting in many ways to the demands of the people to move against some irresponsible acts of the press, and other acts which really I think are unjustified. I think that the act which the Congress has passed on the limitation on political broadcast spending, for instance, sounds good but on the surface poses many dangers to the freedom of the press itself.

We hear a lot about whether public rhetoric is further dividing the country and whether or not the rhetoric of Vice-President Agnew or whomever it may be on radio, television, and newspapers divides the country. Now it is my contention that the country is already divided; there is no question that we have great divisions within our own ranks today, not as a result of what any one man has said, but as a result of a growing unrest across the country over a period of years. On the question of which issues have divided the people, with students it has been seen largely as a matter of the war in Vietnam; but on the other hand more than 50 percent of the student disturbances have been unconnected with Vietnam—over issues ranging from black studies to campus administration and other subjects. So I think there is a real danger in trying to place the burden of all these evils and unrest on the media, and there is a real danger in trying to place this responsibility on an administration, on repression, or on rhetoric or on any one subject. We would profit more from self-examination, and especially for the media themselves to examine in what direction they are going.

Certainly American society today has a credibility problem, and I know that many students especially look with a great deal of skepticism on what is said by a government official. And I think that this is a healthy skepticism, something which has, I believe, strengthened the country and built its minds. Certainly there is also a great number of problems with the press and its own credibility. In 1970, the Associated Press managing editors, who were meeting in Honolulu, released a study which indicated that more than 50 percent of the people had doubt as to the accuracy and validity of what they were reading in their newspapers. Yet there is no question that the press we have today, whether it be printed or broadcast, is the strongest and the best this country has ever known, and certainly the strongest and the best that this world has ever seen. And so we have a very hard question as to how you preserve both freedom and responsibility in the press. We have a strong, free press, a press which has the mechanical ability to transmit sound and sight in almost instant fashion, a press which has made a great technical gain yet in the process of doing so has lost credibility with many of those who read it, with many of those who view and hear it. And I believe that the path back can only be one of constructive introspection by the press itself.

We are encouraged by many of the cooperative efforts we have had from both the broadcast and the print media. For example, one of the things which the media have plunged into heavily has been an effort to provide further education through entertainment programs and through series and documentaries on the problems of narcotics. And you have to look at narcotics as also being connected with some of the violence we see. For example, 45 percent of those in prison for violent crimes in the District of Columbia have a problem of drug addiction, and so certainly some responsibility must be traced to the relationship between the problem of drugs and the problem of violence.

Under our constitutional government, the role of government with regard to the media is, and ought to remain, a limited one. But the role of the government with regard to violence ought to be an activist one. And we will remember, I hope, that as long as we have violence we will need laws to deal with violence, and as long as we have laws to deal with violence we will need effective enforcement tools to back them up. It is certainly a great advantage to have the laws which have been provided thus far by the Congress. The government can react with regard to violence, but it takes more. President Nixon realizes that more is needed than just new laws, new judges, and new prisons. Indeed, he believes that society itself has joined together in both horror and revulsion and with a determination to stop violent acts. He believes that every institution has a role to play in making our society a better one and a more peaceful one. Presidents can act against violence, they can ask for laws, they can inveigh against violence, they can summon the nation to assert itself against the danger. But there are no buttons to push, no levers to pull. The final repository of freedom lies with the people of America; in them it has been vested and in them it must remain. Our democracy can see no other course. Or as Mark Twain once put it, "No country can be well governed, unless its citizens as a body keep religiously before their minds that they are the guardians of the law, that the law officers are only the machinery for its excution."

Violence is not today's way of life, nor will it be a fixture of tomorrow. Our country is yet to be doomed to that destiny, and I don't think it will be. But the violence that exists is intolerable to the nation's health, and curable not alone by the President but by you and me, by the media and the public, by the whole nation. When you look at the great power of the media today, which can make almost any event a very personal one, we can see the great opportunity which lies ahead for better use of the media in helping to get at the heart of the problem of violence. The media have made this war a very personal one, so by television you can see almost the very acts of shooting as they occur in Vietnam. The media have demonstrated their ability to educate—we find for instance, that one of the outstanding programs for children is *Sesame Street*, a program of great impact. It is the media which have the ability to bring election issues to the forefront, to educate the people as to what the chief point of those issues is today. And it is the media which can take you to the moon and allow you to see a man step from the surface of a small projectile and scatter the dust of the moon before your eyes. It is the media which have the power for good as well as for evil—witness the new program of ABC, which seeks to find new means of exploring not only what is wrong but also what is right in a very interesting way. It is the media which have all of the power of selection, and so in the half-hour of national television news you see, a few minutes devoted to each subject determines what you learn about the events of the day.

Ten years ago John Kennedy said we would go to the moon as a nation, and it seemed idealistic and something that we really couldn't comprehend. Yet here we are today, looking at the fact that within that period of ten years not only have we gone to the moon, but we have seen people live beneath the sea, and we have seen ourselves make great conquests in medical science and in so many other fields of technical endeavor. I believe that with the determination of the people, with the determination of the media, and with a government determined not to interfere but to cooperate, we can achieve those kinds of lofty goals ahead. So I conclude by acknowledging that violence is a major problem in the country today, but I am confident that violence need not be prevailing two or three years from now. We are united in pursuit of the same high goals, with the same determination which John Kennedy expressed on reaching toward the moon, that we will conquer this problem by logic and by persuasion.

quinn tamm

5

THE POLICE

Introduction: During the 1968 presidential campaign the "law and order" issue came politically into its own. "Crime is rising nine times faster than the population" was a stock punch line in Richard Nixon's all-purpose campaign speech; Hubert Humphrey struggled desperately and not very successfully to deny Spiro Agnew's accusation that he was "soft on law and order"; and George Wallace never failed to warn his listeners that they might get hit on the head on the way home by a thug who would probably be out of jail before they got out of the hospital. The issue is likely to remain with us throughout the 1970s.

Quinn Tamm has been executive director of the International Association of Chiefs of Police since 1962. From 1934 through 1961 he served as special agent, inspector, and assistant director in the FBI, working in the bureau's identification, training and inspection, and laboratory divisions.

No one denies that crime has been rising alarmingly, but the political dividends to be derived from the crime scare—and the dividends in appropriations for police departments and the FBI—continue to tempt politicians and law enforcement officials to manipulate statistics so as to maximize their quotient of public terror. Notorious among such warping devices has been the FBI's annually published "crime clocks," which graphically portray the shrinking average interval between the commission of various offenses across the country. Since population increase alone would cause these intervals to shrink even in the absence of rising crime, criminologists have consistently denounced them, but with little effect. Ramsey Clark once demonstrated his contempt for such statistics by answering his own rhetorical question: "What do we know when we are told that there is a murder every 43 minutes and a rape every 19? If that time clock applied to the Virgin Islands, everyone there would be murdered in five years, after having been raped twice."

In the essay that follows, Quinn Tamm, a former FBI official himself, succumbs briefly to this popular temptation to base crime rates on time rather than on population, but for the most part his chilling data are responsible and convincing. He echoes Herbert Klein in complaining about the media's close attention to radical militants, and he joins Milton Eisenhower in calling for stricter gun controls. He nowhere alludes to police brutality, however, and his categorical rejection of "illegal acts based on political dissent" as just another form of "criminal activity" would presumably extend from the Weathermen to Martin Luther King. Still, he would recognize that the modern transformation of the image of the American policeman from that of a jovial

Irish cop walking his beat to that of a mechanized and heavily armed "pig" patroling enemy territory is an ominous harbinger of where our urban society is headed.

AS EXECUTIVE DIRECTOR OF THE International Association of Chiefs of Police, my attitudes toward violence, and particularly violent crime, naturally reflect the perspective of the law enforcement official. Violence in its many forms is a very real and personal problem to the nation's police officer, partly because it is so frequently directed against him and partly because of his professional responsibility for maintaining peace and order.

If you have any doubt that we have become a violent society, I direct your attention to the Uniform Crime Reports for the United States. This publication shows that during 1969 almost 5 million major offenses were reported to law enforcement agencies. These offenses—including murder, forcible rape, aggravated assault, burglary, theft over fifty dollars in value, and automobile theft—are among the most serious and are commonly used to indicate the relative incidence of criminal activity. Offenses in these categories increased almost 12 percent during 1969 over the previous year and continued a consistently upward trend which began entirely too many years ago.

Since 1960 the population of the United States has increased 13 percent. During the same period crime has increased 148 percent. This means that major offenses are increasing at more than eleven times the rate of increase of our population. Stated in different terms, our crime rate—the number of offenses per capita population—has more than doubled during the past ten years.

During 1969, almost 15,000 Americans were murdered. An additional 300,000 were assaulted with deadly weapons or in a manner which was calculated to inflict death or serious bodily harm. More than 36,000 forcible rapes occurred and almost 300,000 robberies were committed. A total of 655,000 crimes against persons were reported. In each of these the loss of human life was an imminent possibility.

Crimes against property—which would be excluded as crimes of violence only under the most arbitrary of definitions—have shown a similar increase. While man's home may be his castle, he is unfortunately not protected against the criminal act within its confines. Almost 2 million burglaries occurred during 1969. Briefly, a burglary is the breaking and entering of a building with the intent to steal or commit some other crime. Major thefts not associated with burglaries totaled more than 1½ million. Additionally, almost 900,000 automobiles were stolen.

As unsettling as these figures are, they somehow have a tendency to lose meaning simply because of their magnitude. Reduced to more understandable terms, they mean that for each 13,700 persons alive on January 1, 1969, 1 was murdered during the year; for each 5,500 persons, 1 was the victim of a forcible rape; for each 700 persons, 1 was the victim of an armed robbery; for each 650 persons, 1 was assaulted with sufficient force to create the possibility of his serious injury or death; for each 230 persons, 1 had an automobile belonging to him stolen; for each 130 persons, 1 was the victim of a theft, the value of which exceeded fifty dollars; and 1 person in 200 was the victim of a burglary.

During 1969, nine index crimes—those enumerated above—were committed each minute. Every thirty-six minutes a person was murdered. A forcible rape occurred every fourteen minutes. Every two minutes a person was the victim of an aggravated assault. During the same period of time a person was robbed. An automobile was stolen every thirty-five seconds, and every twenty-one seconds a major theft was committed. To complete the timetable, a burglary occurred every sixteen seconds.

Statistics—even those associated with human suffering—can be something less than impressive. I am sure that if we could find some way to communicate the total human agony and hope lost by crime, we could begin to awaken the kind of public awareness and concern which must exist before we can begin to bring under control the acts of the criminal.

As disturbing as these figures are, they only begin to show the extent to which violence has become a part of our everyday lives. In the mid-1960s, we saw a rebirth of a form of violence which had been largely absent from the American scene for several years. We saw massive civil disorder used to effect social change and influence political decisions. The 1965 riot in the Watts section of Los Angeles was the first in an almost constant succession of major disorders which continued unabated until 1968 and which are still occurring in lesser numbers even today. In the months and years following Watts the major city without riot experience became the exception rather than the rule. Before the tide of street riot began to subside, more than 400 major conflicts had occurred. One hundred ninety-one persons had been killed, 9,216 had been injured, and property damage estimated at almost a billion dollars had been inflicted.

While street incidents with a potential for disaster continue to occur throughout the country, the police have been able to bring the more recent ones under control before they spread to unmanageable proportions. The end of the era of the street riot, however, did not mark the beginning of a time of peace and tranquillity. Instead, the locus of riot changed from the street to the college campus, and we saw the basic tactics of the street rioter being adapted and adopted by the student militant. The seizure of college buildings, the taking as hostages of college administrators, and the disruption of academic routines became the pattern throughout the nation. On frequent occasions, members of the faculty joined the student militants in their rebellion against the education system. College administrators, who had been among the most vocal critics of law enforcement for its handling of riots, were given an opportunity to practice the theories they had expounded. Unfortunately they proved to be no more effective in maintaining peace and order than had the policemen of earlier days.

The taking of hostages proved to be an effective method of attracting attention and has in recent months been utilized in widely separated areas of the world. In Jordan, all passengers of several major airlines flights have been seized. In Canada, public figures have been kidnapped and murdered. In Latin America, United States officials have been abducted and killed. In Turkey, American servicemen have been seized for ransom. Unless we are effective in our efforts to combat this type of violence, it may well become the theme of the 1970s. If the militant activist is able to gain that which he seeks by taking hostages with the threat of death, this type of incident will become the tool which he will use with increasing frequency. If, however, we have the courage to refuse to negotiate for the release of persons held prisoner, the ineffectiveness of this form of pressure will soon become apparent and it will come to an end.

In recent months we have seen a tremendous increase in the number and severity of attacks on police officers. Because this type of violence was obviously on the increase and because accurate data were not being collected and disseminated on a planned basis, the International Association of Chiefs of Police and the Law Enforcement Assistance Administration of the United States Department of Justice cooperated in the establishment of a national Bomb Data Center and a Police Weapons Center. As a part of these programs, information is now being collected regarding the number of attacks on and resultant deaths of the nation's police. Additionally, the number of incidents in which explosive and incendiary devices are used is determined. The centers began operation in July 1970, so statistics for the first six months of that year are not available. However, those collected during the fall of 1970 are justification for great concern. From July 1 through October the center received reports of 751 assaults on policemen. Thirty-one police officers were murdered as a result of these assaults. A total of 509 incidents in which explosive and incendiary devices were used to disrupt public order were reported. This type of violence has frequently been directed against agencies of the criminal justice system. In Cambridge, Maryland, a section of a courthouse was destroyed by explosion. In Des Moines, Iowa, and Shaker Heights, Ohio, bombs either destroyed or seriously damaged the police facilities. Police departments throughout the country, already undermanned because of a rising crime rate, have been forced to assign a part of their manpower to guard duty at police stations and other governmental facilities.

Many of the recent attacks on the police officer have been made not because of who he is but simply because of what he is. Sniper attacks, ambushings, terrorist bombings, and other assaults on police officers have become a grave threat to the very foundation of our system of government. The officer is now the object of attack not because of enforcement activity, not because of the necessity of mediating tense situations in our society, but because he stands as the most visible representation of the authority of society.

An officer in Omaha, Nebraska, was killed and seven others wounded when an explosive charge in a suitcase was detonated when the suitcase was moved. In Minneapolis, Minnesota, two patrolmen responded to a telephone plea from a woman who said her sister was having a baby and needed assistance. When the officers were unable to get a response at the address they were given, one went to the rear of the building. He heard a shot and returned to the front to find his partner dead from a high-powered rifle bullet fired from across the street. Investigation showed that although the woman who lived at the address was expecting a child, the time was several months away. In Toledo, two policemen were sitting in a squad car when a man walked up and said, "Hey, baby, here's something for you," and at the same time shot one officer in the head, causing his death. In Chicago, a wounded officer lay in an alley. His assailant approached him, placed the gun to the officer's head, and pulled the trigger. In Detroit, in New York, in Philadelphia, in Baltimore, in Seattle, in Berkeley, and in many other cities throughout the nation, officers have recently been killed solely because they were policemen.

What a change has taken place, particularly here in America, in the attitude of some people toward police. It was not too long ago that an attack on a police officer during a raid or an attempted arrest was front page news. Today these so-called open attacks, as distinguished from sniping, ambushing, or bombing, receive hardly any public notice, even when the attacks result in death. The attitude toward resistance is not limited to the person or persons the officers are attempting to arrest. Our jobs are made doubly dangerous by the fact that some people seem to feel that they have a right to interfere violently with the police and to liberate persons arrested and at the same time by mob action to beat, kick, or shoot the officers. Incredible as this is, this is not really what I am talking about. I am crying out against the "unprovoked attacks," but by doing so I do not in any way condone or excuse the attacks to which officers are subjected in making arrests.

In recent years the training of police officers has reached the point where competent, finely trained men are graduating from police academies qualified to handle a great variety of problems with which law enforcement must deal. What a commentary on our system of criminal justice that we must now concentrate on teaching officers how to avoid sniper attacks, how to spot an ambush, how to react to the danger of a booby trap.

Should the terrorist tactics being practiced against police today be allowed to continue, we will begin to evaluate the successful performance of a tour of duty by whether the officer was able to work his beat for eight hours without being assaulted—or if assaulted, whether he managed to survive. These tactics are threatening the very foundation of our society. All of us are well aware of what would happen to the freedom of our people should those terrorists succeed in removing the police from our streets, and we cannot and will not let that happen.

In the performance of his duties the policeman willingly places himself in a vulnerable position. He voluntarily exposes himself to hazards which the citizen seldom thinks of and to which he is never exposed. He does this because service to the public frequently demands that he place the safety of others above his own.

However, the officer is not willing to be—and society has no right to ask that he be—the victim of blind and vicious attacks simply because he is the agent of law and order in our modern society. Senseless attacks on the police officer create an intolerable situation and one which must not, cannot, and will not be permitted to continue.

I am not able to provide for you a blueprint which, if followed, will bring an end to the violence so prevalent in our daily lives. I doubt that anywhere such a plan exists or even that one can be developed. The factors which have created the conditions under which we live are highly complex and have developed over a considerable period of time. Solutions—and they must be found—will also be complex, will be composed of many separate efforts, and must be applied over a long period of time. What I am saying is that there is no single program we can undertake which will solve our problems. We must develop many programs, hoping that each will provide some benefit and that in the end the cumulative effect will provide for us the solutions we need.

What, then, are some of the things we can do? I think that high on the list of priorities must be a clarification of the issues involved. We must more consistently substitute thought for emotional reaction. We must make decisions based on calm, logical reasoning. We can begin this by insisting on more valid definitions of terms to which we are constantly subjected. For example, we are frequently told that the rioter, the student activist, the militant is protesting against society's political and legal system and consequently should be viewed as being outside the restrictions imposed by these systems. The suggestion is made that riot, assault, and robbery should be viewed as political acts rather than criminal acts. All sorts of indignities against the social body are being committed in the name of political and social progress. If we fall prey to this type of fallacious reasoning, we create for ourselves problems for which we are not likely to find solutions. We need to realize that while dissent has a very valuable place in our society and that without it we would not progress, dissent must be made within the framework of the law. There can be no more justification for illegal acts based on political dissent than for any other criminal activity. We must view riots as incidents of arson, of burglary, of theft and pillage, of looting, of assaults, and of murder rather than as political in nature.

There are established in our society legal and proper methods for effecting both political and social change. We must insist that those who dissent keep their actions within due bounds, and we must view as being basically criminal in nature any action which is outside those limits.

We are warned of the dangers of polarization of our society to the extent that we are perhaps persuaded that any disagreement is contrary to the public welfare. It is even suggested to us that support of law and order by the police officer is undesirable because it may soldify opposition and may cause those who disagree to resort to violence. This suggests that the policeman who enforces the law equitably and with justice and who is met with resistance by those who do not choose to obey the law is creating civil unrest. This is the type of thinking we cannot afford to adopt. The breach of public peace is created by the person who refuses to conform to the requirements of the law and not by the policeman who is charged with the responsibility for enforcing it. Occasionally we see public officials who should know better, blame the police for massive civil disturbance which develops when proper law enforcement is applied. We have no right to give our policemen the responsibility for maintaining peace and order and then blame them when certain members of society refuse to obey the law and create disorder.

The nation's press can make a significant contribution to the reduction of violence by adopting a more restrained attitude in its handling of the violence which does occur. Freedom of the press is one of the most sacred traditions passed on to us by our forefathers. Neither I personally nor the International Association of Chiefs of Police collectively would ever want to see that freedom suppressed.

I would, however, like to challenge anyone in the news media—either newspapers, television, or radio—to give me any justification whatsoever for the great exposure being given people who have as their avowed intention the destruction of our way of life. I realize that everything that is news is entitled to be reported, but I strongly question the exposure that was given to the members of the "Chicago Seven," to the Students for a Democratic Society, to the Weathermen, to the Black Panthers, and to those individuals who have indicated a revolutionary trend toward destruction. Without the exposure given by the news media, most of these organizations would cease to exist. They exist both by and for publicity, and without it they would disappear.

Another thing we can do is reduce the time lapse between the commission of an offense and the time the accused is brought to trial. The right to a speedy trial, guaranteed in the Bill of Rights, was originally designed as a protection to the citizen. But elaborate defenses and overburdened courts have combined effectively to deny this basic right, which society must now reclaim. I ask you, where is the wisdom of waiting for months before bringing the defendant to trial?

Before I am accused of proposing kangaroo justice, let me hasten to add that I agree with the philosophy that a man is innocent until he is found guilty in a court of competent jurisdiction. I do not advocate that we convict all persons who are brought to trial. While I think the police of our nation are generally very efficient in their investigations and in their filing of cases, I think that being human they can occasionally err. I think justice demands a continuation of a court system free and independent to preserve the guarantees of individual freedom and liberty. However, I am convinced that a failure to handle properly those who have been convicted of the most serious violations cannot avoid damaging the fabric of our society.

We are beginning to hear more and more voices raised in support of increased legislation designed to control violence. Some persons are proposing that all assaults on our nation's police be made federal crimes. I am not at all sure that this is the direction in which effectiveness lies. While there is in some areas a need for additional legislation, I think we have seen that on most occasions new laws do not necessarily provide solutions to the problems for which they were created. In most instances, acceptable solutions perhaps lie in the more effective utilization of laws which already exist.

In one area, however, there is a need for investigation to determine whether additional legislation is indicated. We are hearing charges and denials that the attacks on police officers are or are not the result of a conspiracy. I think a part of the problem is a lack of definition by those who are taking stands in this respect. At our recent annual conference, members of the IACP adopted a resolution which noted the increased frequency of personal attacks upon police officers and observed that these attacks have occurred because of the official nature of the duties being performed by the officer. The membership felt that an attack upon a police officer or upon a public official is in effect an attack upon the entire social order and that such assaults violate the federally protected rights of a specific group of citizens. They also stated a belief that a number of attacks have been planned and executed by those traveling in interstate commerce or by those using a facility of interstate commerce. They observed that the investigation of the incidents is often difficult and sometimes impossible for local authorities to perform because of the interstate activity of the attackers.

It was our unanimous resolution that the Congress of the United States be urged to enact legislation making it a federal crime to injure or kill a police officer of any jurisdiction because of his official character by one acting in interstate commerce or one using a facility of interstate commerce. It was further recommended that legislation be enacted to provide that every assassination of a police officer which occurs because of his official performance of duties be viewed as involving interstate commerce unless evidence establishing its purely local nature could be developed. It concluded that the investigation of such crimes be made jointly by local and federal authorities, and it provided that the department for which the officer worked could request federal assistance, which the federal agency then would be required to provide.

I think there is a definite need for additional legislation in one particular area, and that is in gun control. It seems to me that one method by which we can begin to bring violence under control is by controlling the weapons with which violence is most often committed. The press and public have vehemently debated the pros and cons of gun controls for several years. Some articles and discussions have been objective; others have been based more on emotion than on fact. Passage of the Omnibus Crime Control and Safe Streets Act of 1968, with its section providing for federal control of certain types of firearms, has stimulated additional interest in the problem.

I think we need to ask ourselves one fundamental question: can gun controls help preserve law and order and protect the public peace? The answer to this seemingly simple question is multifaceted and far more complex than one might expect on superficial examination. But, on balance, the answer is *yes*—if the controls are carefully devised in consultation with professional law enforcement officers.

The IACP in 1922 recommended federal legislation to regulate interstate shipment of weapons and thus to eliminate the availability of all types of firearms to anyone not having legitimate reasons to possess them. During the same year, the IACP proposed the enactment of uniform state laws which would:

1. Require each person, firm, or corporation to be licensed before selling weapons.
2. Provide that all persons licensed report in detail to local police authorities any weapons sold, their descriptions and serial numbers, by whom purchased, and for what reason.
3. Forbid anyone to purchase, possess, or carry a weapon without a permit to do so granted by local police authorities.
4. Stipulate that all permits to carry weapons include a complete description and left thumb print of the permit holder.
5. Ensure absolute uniformity in applications, licenses, and per-

mits by providing that the secretary of state or some other suitable state official furnish all blanks for this purpose to those authorized to have them and that he keep a central record for the entire state of all purchases and sales of weapons and all permits issued.

6. Stipulate that local authorities also keep records of all purchases and sales of weapons and of all permits issued within their respective jurisdictions.

A review of these recommendations and the recent proliferation of the use of firearms in illegal activities show them to be needed even more today than when they were first proposed. More and more people are acquiring guns at a time when crime rates continue to rise and violence has become an everyday occurrence.

It seems to me that society can benefit from more restrictive gun controls in a variety of ways. First, simple logic tells us that if guns were less readily available to potential murderers and assassins, the incidence of death from these causes would be reduced. As I remarked earlier, in 1969 14,590 murders were committed in the United States. Firearms continued to be the predominant weapon used in murder, with 65 percent of the reported murders committed with this type of weapon. Homicide is generally held to be a crime of passion, with the vast majority of offenses committed in the heat of the moment. The carefully planned murder is the exception rather than the rule. It seems to me indisputable that if we are able to make firearms less readily available the tempers of many potential murderers will cool before they can find some other effective weapon, and as a result the number of homicides will be reduced.

A second way in which adequate gun controls can help the police is by making theirs a less hazardous profession. A very large percentage of the recent assaults on police officers have been committed with firearms. During 1969, murders of police officers were the highest in history at eighty-six. Of these, eighty-three, or 97 percent, were committed with firearms. Any legislation which would make less readily available to the criminal a weapon with which to commit an assault would inevitably reduce the danger which has become so much a part of the policeman's everyday life. Not only would the safety of the officer be increased but also the safety of the citizen. Criminals, unfortunately, are not preoccupied with avoiding injury to innocent persons in their efforts to gain their illegal objectives. When members of a mob possess firearms and start shooting, innocent persons who are not participating in the disorder must inevitably be injured; hysteria spreads more rapidly and restoration of order is much more difficult.

This suggests a third way in which adequate gun controls can help preserve law and order. Fewer lives would be lost and disorders would be brought under control sooner if guns were not so readily available to actual and potential activists dedicated to destroying our society through violent and destructive mass action. There have been cases when the idly curious who came to a scene of civil disorder armed for their protection have fired after others started to shoot and panic began to spread.

Fourth, with adequate gun controls a better supply of firearms would be available for purchase at reasonable prices by those with legitimate requirements for them. There have been incidents in which police agencies have experienced difficulty in obtaining firearms for issue to police officers. Because of a demand for weapons, prices are high and police agencies sometimes have to wait months before their orders can be filled. Some years ago I was told by a leading firearms broker that he was not able to meet the demands of retail gun dealers who were pressed by purchase requests not from professional law enforcement officers but from the general public. There is a legitimate place for firearms in America today, but there is something seriously amiss when hand guns are more readily available to the general public than to the law enforcement agencies, which are staffed by professionals trained in judicious control and effective use of weapons. I am convinced that the right kind of gun control can help preserve law and order and can assist us in our efforts to bring violence more under control.

As a final observation, I suggest the necessity for ensuring that violence does not prove to be the most effective method of bringing about needed change. The so-called establishment should identify those areas in which change is needed and should work toward that change within the framework of the law. Each time we refuse to listen to dissent, then admit its validity by making change after violence has occurred, we promote future violence.

The problems confronting society today are as great as at any time in history. But efforts directed toward finding solutions to those problems are also great. I am confident that dedicated law enforcement agencies working closely with an aroused public can produce viable solutions to our problems.

THE VARIETIES OF
PROTEST AND VIOLENCE

jerome d. frank

6

THE PSYCHOLOGY OF VIOLENCE

Introduction: In recent years a new and controversial body of literature based primarily upon the science of ethology—the scientific study of animal behavior—has resurrected and popularized in such books as Konrad Lorenz's *On Aggression* and Robert Audrey's *The Territorial Imperative* the ancient notion that man is instinctively aggressive. Briefly, this thesis is based upon the observation that evolution encouraged the development and genetic transmission of intraspecific or species-specific aggression, especially among males. This aggression was functional to the survival and prosperity

Jerome D. Frank is professor of psychiatry at The Johns Hopkins University School of Medicine. He received from Harvard his B.A. in 1930, his Ph.D. in psychology in 1934, and his M.D. in 1939. His publications include *Persuasion and Healing: A Comparative Study of Psychotherapy* (Baltimore: Johns Hopkins Press, 1961), and *Sanity and Survival: Psychological Aspects of War and Peace* (New York: Random House, 1967).

of the species because, particularly through defense of territory, it was conducive to the most efficient distribution of the species over the environment available to support it and assured that the most vigorous members would propagate the species. Yet to avoid self-slaughter, the various species—and especially those possessing lethal armaments—developed powerful instinctive restraints and symbolic patterns of combat that spared the lives of the losers.

But primitive man, who was equipped with relatively puny physical weapons, perforce developed a minimal instinctive restraint to bridle his intraspecific aggression. Consequently when his ingenious technology produced weapons capable of massive destruction, he became the planet's most truly dangerous and immoral creature. Hence the cynical Roman epigram, *homo homini lupus* —man is a wolf to man—seemed to represent a libel on the gentle wolf, and the thesis that aggression was innate seemed clearly to reinforce Job's despairing cry that "man is born unto trouble as the sparks fly upward."

It is not surprising, then, that liberal social scientists have deplored the conservative implications of this dim view of human nature. The resurgence of this ancient nature-versus-nurture debate has prompted many of them to deny that innate and physiological impulses are remotely as important as environmental conditions, if indeed they operate at all, in prompting human violence. Here Dr. Jerome Frank faces this question squarely. He readily acknowledges that innate human "programs" for violent responses play a large roll in human behavior. But he also insists that such propensities, unlike the biological compulsions to eat, drink, breathe, and sleep, need never be activated and are subject to the same laws of learning as other forms of behavior. His suggestions as to how violence can be controlled and minimized through surgery, medicine, childrearing, and new institutional arrangements are hopeful, constructive, and—especially in regard to his thoughts concerning greater sexual freedom—most intriguing. But his discussion of the frightening experiment that tested the power of obedience to elicit destructive behavior is rather depressing in a world armed with nuclear missiles aimed at potential victims who are so psychologically remote.

OTHER DISCUSSIONS IN THIS VOLUME have concentrated on collective or group violence and institutional means for its control. This is entirely proper, for it is group violence that today immediately threatens the survival of our society, if not of civilization itself. No matter how large the scale of violence, however, or how impersonal it is, violent acts are all committed by individuals—some person has to throw the punch, wield the knife, fire the gun, or launch the missile. Moreover, while group forces, as we shall see, are far more powerful determinants of behavior than individual motives, the latter cannot be neglected.

Rates of violent crime are higher in some urban areas than others, suggesting that a culture of violence may predispose to crime. But, as Dr. Eisenhower pointed out, in these areas most of the violent acts are committed by repeaters—one study found that 53 percent of the homicides, assaults, and rapes were committed by 6 percent of those interviewed. Apparently thresholds for violence differ among members of a group, and acts of violence, like all behavior, are determined by the interaction of group characteristics with personal qualities of the individual.

Current discussions of determinants of violence are clouded by the old pseudoquestion that has haunted biology and psychology for years: is the propensity for violent behavior innate or acquired? The argument derives its heat from the implicit assumption that if it is innate, nothing can be done about it. Of course, like all behavior, it has both genetic and environmental determinants, and the presence of genetic components does not mean that it cannot be controlled. Programs of violent behavior are built into the structure of the nervous systems of all creatures, including man, and there are undoubtedly innate temperamental differences in the propensity for violence among individual humans. But whether violent behavior actually occurs in any given situation and the form it takes depends on the specific properties of that situation and the life history of the person. These are modifiable.

To be more specific, stimulation of certain brain areas in many different species will elicit patterns of violent behavior, but the kind of behavior that results depends on the situation. The crucial role of the environment has been beautifully demonstrated by a series of experiments on a monkey in which the brain center for violent behavior was stimulated by remote radio command through an implanted electrode. In a colony in which she was the dominant member, she became more aggressive; but in a colony in which she was at the bottom of the social scale, she tried to run away. Stimulation of the identical spot in the brain of the same monkey caused her to fight in one social setting and flee in another. Stimulation of brain centers for violence, furthermore, may lead the animal to search for a suitable target. He will run mazes, open doors, and climb barriers to reach a victim. In men this behavior would be called "spoiling for a fight." Stimulation of these areas apparently creates motivation to attack—that is, the act of attacking becomes pleasant in itself.

Clinical evidence in two human diseases involving brain damage suggests that we have similar centers for violent emotions and behaviors in our brains. The first is the behavior of children who survived the encephalitis epidemic in 1920. "Within a few months . . . a marked destructiveness and impulsiveness often ensued," one report said. "Primitive aggressive and sexual impulses were immediately carried into action, with consequent serious and even murderous attacks on others, but occasionally upon themselves, leading to gruesome self-mutilation."[1] Similarly, some patients with epilepsy caused by damage to certain parts of the brain are quick to take offense, imagine that all references are directed personally against themselves, hold grudges for long periods, and are liable to violent, short-lived, and unprovoked outbursts. The threshold for violent behavior, then, can be lowered by direct stimulation or pathological damage to certain brain areas.

If we are honest with ourselves, most of us will admit that, even though our brains are intact, if we are sufficiently frightened or angered the urge to attack may become almost overwhelming. This is implicitly acknowledged by the strict rules setting permissible limits to violence in body contact sports.

Glenn Gray, in his perceptive book *The Warriors*, describes his own feelings as he emerged from the trenches to attack the Germans in World War I:

I was boiling with a mad rage, which had taken hold of me and all the others in an incomprehensible fashion. The overwhelming wish to kill gave wings to my feet. Rage pressed bitter tears from my eyes. The monstrous desire for annihilation, which hovered over the battlefield, thickened the brains of the men and submerged them in a red fog. We called to each other in sobs and stammered disconnected sentences. A neutral observer might have perhaps believed that we were seized by an excess of happiness.[2]

He adds: ". . . Thousands of youths who never suspected the presence of such an impulse in themselves have learned in military life the mad excitement of destroying."

Mention of soldiers, who are young men, is a reminder that an important biological determinant of the propensity to violence is the male sex hormone. In all species of animals males castrated before puberty are less prone to fight than those allowed to mature sexually. Males of species whose production of the male sex hor-

[1] D. Hill, in J. D. Carthy and F. J. Ebling (eds.), *The National History of Aggression* (London and New York: Academic Press, 1964), p. 93.
[2] Gray, *The Warriors: Reflections on Men in Battle* (New York: Harper & Row, 1959), p. 52.

mone fluctuates periodically are much more combative during the mating season when the level is high. There are no analogous data on humans, but it is suggestive that powerful aggressive drives are generally believed to go with strong sexual ones. The "machismo" of Latin Americans includes both agressive and sexual prowess, and the aggressive heroes of myth and literature are characteristically highly sexed, from "hairy chested Achilles," who precipitated the tragedy of the Iliad because Agamemnon stole his girl, to James Bond and Mike Hammer.

In this connection a thought-provoking finding of cross-cultural studies is a high correlation between punishment of extramarital sex relations and bellicosity, incidence of personal crime, and killing, torturing, or mutilating enemies. On the not unreasonable assumption that societies disapproving extramarital intercourse have generally restrictive sexual standards with resulting sexual frustration, this finding suggests that violence may be one way of relieving sexual tensions.

Before leaving the "innate" biological propensities to violence, let me emphasize that in the intact healthy brain, centers inhibiting violent behavior are fully as strong as those releasing it, nor is there any biological need that these centers be activated. In contrast to biological needs such as eating and breathing, in the absence of appropriate environmental instigators an animal can go through life without ever fighting and its health will not suffer in the least. Furthermore, violent behavior obeys the same laws of learning as other forms of behavior, in animals as well as in humans. Members of the same biological strain of mice can be trained to be vicious fighters or absolute pacifists. Especially interesting, in view of its possible relevance to child-rearing, is that failure to stimulate violent behavior in infant animals reduces their combativeness as adults, as if the propensity atrophies through disuse.

In man, situational determinants of the frequency, intensity, and forms of violent behavior far outweigh biological ones and can be conveniently grouped into two broad categories—early life experiences and instigators in the immediate situation.

Children learn violence through imitation, reward and punishment, and repeated exposure to stimuli that arouse it. Thus some impulsive murderers have undergone especially painful and frightening experiences in early life, particularly continuous, remorseless brutality by both parents or by one with compliant acquiescence by the other. Pain and threat are both powerful instigators of violence, and a child brought up in such a home would experience large amounts of both. Furthermore, he is confronted with a model of violent behavior, and imitation is a very effective way to learn.

Along the same lines, a comparative study of delinquent and nondelinquent middle class, adolescent boys has shown that children whose families freely use corporal punishment are more aggressive than those whose families use nonviolent methods of discipline. The former have frequently experienced pain but are not allowed to attack its source, so they must seek outside targets —an activity that may be reinforced by parental approval. In addition, the physically aggressive parent affords a model for imitation. At the other end of the spectrum, children disciplined by nonviolent means are not rewarded for violence and do not have violent models to imitate, and in addition their impulses to violence may atrophy through disuse.

The power of imitation to shape behavior is relevant to the controversy over the effect on children of viewing violence on television and in films. The reader is probably aware that today many children spend more time in front of the TV set than they do in school. Albert Bandura, a psychologist, has done a brilliant series of studies with nursery school children in which he has demonstrated that they readily imitate violent behavior shown by an aggressive model on what seems to them to be a TV screen. If the aggressive model wins, he is emulated more frequently than if he is punished. An especially disquieting finding is that they emulate the winner even if they label his behavior as bad and resolve the resulting conflict by derogating the victim. Too many films and TV programs teach children that the world is a violent and untrustworthy place and demonstrate a variety of violent techniques for coping with this frustrating, hostile environment. It seems incredible to me that this repeated exposure would not have some influence on subsequent attitudes and behavior.

The most common instigators to violence are actual or symbolic threats to the integrity or survival of the organism. Humans, because of their capacity to symbolize, respond to the meanings of events rather than to the events themselves, so a person may respond as violently to an insult, a symbolic attack on his self-esteem, as to a bodily assault. The concept of frustration can be stretched to cover most causes of violence, since anything that impedes the progress of a person to his goals is ultimately a threat to his survival. Conflict is especially frustrating since each antagonist is interfering with the efforts of the other to achieve his goals and, in addition, it involves threats or attacks.

Violence, then, is an adaptive mechanism—a means of coping with frustration. It is, in a sense, the last resort. If it fails, one has no other recourse, so he gives up and becomes apathetic. Both violence and apathy characterize oppressed segments of our society.

I should now like to consider three instigators to violence which seem especially relevant to the problems of today. Two, relative deprivation and the sense of powerlessness, are forms of frustration. The third, obedience, belongs in a different category but may be the most ominous of all.

The term "relative deprivation" refers to the gap between what one has and what one believes himself entitled to. This seems to be at least as provocative as the absolute level of deprivation, probably more so. The denizens of the streets of Calcutta, for example, have an immeasurably lower standard of living than American blacks in urban ghettos. Yet they accept their lot with apathetic resignation, while many blacks explode in rage and frustration.

Blacks in American slums have been raised in a society that professes equal justice under law and equality of opportunity for all. Yet this society has steadfastly refused to grant either right to blacks and has oppressed them in many other ways—often, to be sure, out of indifference rather than malice. But the discrepancy between promises and reality is nonetheless glaring, and those who experience it most keenly seem to be the most prone to violence. Thus the most destructive ghetto riots in recent years have broken out in the least impoverished black communities such as Detroit and Watts, possibly because their inhabitants had more hope than blacks in more economically depressed cities and therefore felt more keenly the gaps between their living standard and that of the surrounding white community. Similarly the rioter, as compared with the nonrioter, has been shown over and over again to be the person who experiences relative deprivation most keenly. In addition to being a young male, which may reflect the hormonal factor, he is better educated than the average inner city Negro but can get only menial jobs and intermittent employment. He feels strongly that he deserves a better job but is barred from it by discrimination. He hates whites, but on socioeconomic more than racial grounds—that is, he hates middle-class Negroes just as much. He envies the middle class as the group he wishes to join but also resents it as the impeder of his upward progress. Along the same lines, he is substantially better informed about politics than the nonrioter. One writer has summed him up as having had just enough of a taste of a better life to want more but not being able to get it.

A particularly severe form of frustration is a sense of powerlessness, an inability to get anyone to pay attention. One of the few sound insights of the Marquis de Sade was that one of the greatest satisfactions in life lies in getting a response from someone else and that the only sure way of forcing him to respond is to hurt him. Similarly, interviews with violent people in deprived areas always elicit the same theme, which can be summed up in the statement of a twenty-five-year-old Negro man: "You got to prove you got power or you ain't nothing." A twenty-seven-year-old Negro woman said: "Look, you live your life from the very beginning with everything and everyone controllin' you. You can't do nothin' but just take it. Then you start saying 'I'm gonna start controllin'.' You control property by stealin', you control people by hittin'."[3] Violence for such persons is the last resort, the final way of trying to exert some influence on the environment after all else fails.

Among the most powerful instigators of violent behavior is one that is generally overlooked because it is usually considered in other contexts. This is obedience to legitimate authority, a characteristic that is deeply ingrained in members of all organized societies—in fact, the stability of the social system depends on it. We are inclined to carry out orders, no matter what they are, including orders to commit destructive acts, if we accept the authority of the person who gives the commands.

The power of obedience to elicit destructive behavior was demonstrated by a series of ingenious and frightening experiments conducted by Stanley Milgram. Ostensibly they were studies of the effect of punishment on learning. One subject, who acted as the teacher, was instructed to give progressively more severe shocks to another, the learner, in response to errors he made in a learning task. The maximum shock was ostensibly 480 volts, which is in the dangerous range.

Let me explain that the learner or victim was, of course, an accomplice and no shocks were actually administered. Moreover, the experimenter was acutely aware of the ethical implications of this study and went to great lengths to forestall or counteract any possible harmful effects on the subjects.

It was found that the more remote the victim was psychologically, the larger the proportion of subjects giving the maximum shock. If he was in an adjoining room and protested only once by pounding on the wall, two-thirds of the subjects—who were, let me emphasize, normal American adults—went up to the maximum

---

[3] Blair Justice, *Violence in the City* (Fort Worth: Texas Christian University Press, 1969), p. 67.

shock in response to the experimenter's urgings. When the victim was in plain sight and the subject had to hold his hand on the shock plate despite his struggles and screams, the proportion giving the maximum shock fell to one-third—still uncomfortably high. It was as if they had entrusted their consciences to the experimenter, who represented authority.

A finding with especially disquieting implications was that if the subject simply had to throw a master switch which enabled someone else to give the shock, compliance rose to over 90 percent. That is, inhibitions practically vanished if responsibility was diffused.

The conditions producing the highest rate of obedience are uncomfortably similar to those that prevail in a Polaris submarine or in a missile bunker. To fire the missile requires the cooperation of several people. No one person is completely responsible, and the victim is psychologically very remote. So it is scarcely surprising that a Polaris submarine commander, when asked how it felt to be the man whose act could unleash the submarine's destructive power, replied that he had never given it any thought but that if he ever had to hit, he would hit and there wouldn't be a second's hesitation.

Lest this sketchy review of some of the causes of individual violence be merely an academic exercise, let me close with a brief consideration of some implications for its control. Control of the biological determinants of violence requires direct interventions into the functioning of the brain. Although this may conjure up an Orwellian nightmare, removal of damaged brain areas in patients subject to bursts of violent behavior is proving highly successful. A recent estimate is that about one-fourth of such patients are treatable by this means.

A more subtle approach is to implant electrodes in those areas, monitor their electrical waves, and program a computer to send an inhibitory impulse by radio when they show a pattern indicating that an eruption of violence is imminent. This has been done with a monkey, and the inventor of the process is already toying with the idea of using it to forestall epileptic attacks in humans.

Turning to medications, agents that block the physiological action of the male sex hormone have a powerful calming effect on violence-prone male epileptics. It looks as if the male hormone sensitizes the centers for violence in diseased brains, which would be consistent with the apparent relationship between virility and aggressiveness in persons with intact brains that I mentioned earlier. There is no evidence today, however, that surgical intervention, remote electrical stimulation, or hormonal blocking agents have any effect on violence in persons whose brains are intact. But who knows what research will discover in the future?

As to other medications, certain tranquilizing agents in widespread use seem to inhibit violence in the normal population. Of these heroin, of course, is the most powerful. Since the use of this drug is associated with a high crime rate, this statement may be surprising, but of course the heroin addict commits crimes only to get the money to support his very expensive habit. He prefers to steal and becomes violent only when the drug's effects are wearing off and he is desperate. Indirect evidence that heroin inhibits violence is that the rising use of this drug has been accompanied by a sharp decline in gang warfare. The use of heroin to inhibit violence would be an obvious example of a cure being worse than the disease. But many tranquilizers, by reducing general irritability, may have a similar, although less pronounced, effect. Perhaps the tons of tranquilizers consumed by Americans in part reflect attempts to dampen violent reactions to an excessively irritating environment.

The main hope for reducing the level of violence in society to a tolerable level, however, lies in reducing its psychological and socioeconomic instigators and creating more effective institutions for its control. How to accomplish these goals lies outside the purview of this discussion, but our review suggests what some of them should be.

For the long run, methods of child-rearing that socialize children by giving or withholding praise rather than by corporal punishment should be encouraged. Our educational curricula, which now glorify successful practitioners of violence—that is, war heroes—should glorify heroes of peace instead, including great writers and scientists and especially fighters for social justice who have held themselves and their followers to militant nonviolence, such as Mohandas K. Gandhi and Martin Luther King. Along the same lines, as already suggested, reduction of violence in television and motion pictures could certainly do no harm and might contribute to a more peaceful citizenry.

These are for the long pull. Measures to control violence that could have immediate effect involve, on the one hand, more effective use of negative sanctions—less provocative use of police power, more efficient administration of justice, reform of the prison system, and the like—and, on the other, reduction of the instigators to violence which I have lumped under the term "relative deprivation."

A knotty aspect of attempts to improve the economic, educational, and political position of the underprivileged is that expectations rise as fast as or faster than actual gains, so that the gap between them, and therefore the sense of relative deprivation, does not necessarily diminish. But efforts to improve the lot of the oppressed that involve them actively in the process, thereby combating their sense of powerlessness, have already been shown to diminish resort to violence. In any case, programs that open the future, as it were, should help to reduce the sense of frustration that instigates violence.

Improvement of law enforcement and correction of social injustice are amply discussed by other contributors to this volume, so I shall move on to other potential means of reducing or controlling violence that have received less attention.

One lies in the development of alternate, nondestructive ways for satisfying needs now met by violence. Among these might be greater sexual freedom. At least the cross-cultural study showing a very high relationship between an index of sexual frustration and violence suggests this line of thought. Perhaps the current trend toward permissiveness with respect to sexual behavior will in time reduce the amount of violence in the young. Certainly many flower children are both sexually uninhibited and remarkably peaceful. Phenomena such as the Manson "family" are reminders that we do not know enough about the conditions under which sex inhibits or instigates violence. In the meanwhile, it may well be that under some conditions the slogan "make love, not war" is psychologically sound.

Turning to more direct substitutes for violence, a ground for hope is that human beings, because of their symbolic powers, have an extraordinary capacity to satisfy the same need in many different ways. Vicarious or symbolic ways of expressing impulses to violence in socially harmless forms already exist. Perhaps they could be further developed. Spectator sports are an example, even though under some circumstances they provoke spectators to violent confrontations. More hopeful would be exploitation of new opportunities for manifesting heroism and other manly virtues, which in the past have been characteristically linked to violence. These include especially exploration of outer space and the undersea world. Although only a few persons can participate directly, many millions do so vicariously through their television sets and, perhaps, gain a sense of reflected glory.

But probably the greatest hope lies in the creation of group norms that condemn violence instead of glorifying it. For group standards are more powerful determinants of human behavior than biological needs, including that of self-preservation. This was forcefully demonstrated by the siege of Leningrad in which hundreds of thousands of people starved to death in the presence of ample supplies of nourishing food. The trouble was that the nourishment happened to be human flesh, and for the vast majority of the citizenry starvation was preferable to cannibalism. More pertinent to this discussion is that many nonviolent fighters in the movements led by Gandhi and King preferred to die rather than to defend themselves by violence. These great leaders were able to create group standards, which unfortunately proved to be only temporary, that held their followers to nonviolence in the face of provocation as extreme as any faced by soldiers in battle.

As these movements have confirmed, obedience is a very powerful shaper of behavior. This suggests, finally, that perhaps the most promising way to achieve control of violence would be to focus on the world's leaders. It is abundantly clear that violence is becoming increasingly ineffectual and dangerous as a means of solving both domestic and international conflicts, but statesmen cling to it because they have no faith in other forms of power. What is needed is not only to convince them that resort to violence will not solve their problems, which is easy, but that other measures will work better, which is impossible because effective alternatives for achieving the ends now sought by violence have not yet been devised. If they existed, leaders, instead of ordering their followers to commit acts of violence, would forbid them to do so. Then our problems would be largely solved.

Modern developments in mass communication, transportation, and other features of modern technology have created new possibilities for developing effective nonviolent ways of waging or controlling conflict. It is high time that politicians, jurists, economists, communications experts, behavioral scientists, and other experts in human behavior gave the highest priority to the achievement of this goal. Nothing less will enable civilization to survive.

STUDIES MENTIONED IN THE TEXT

Bandura, A., Ross, D., and Ross, S. A. 1963. Imitation of Film-Mediated Aggressive Models. *J. Abn. and Soc. Psychology,* 66: 3–11.

Bandura, A., and Walters, R. H. 1959. *Adolescent Aggression.* New York: Ronald Press.

Delgado, J. M. R. 1967. Social Rank and Radio-Stimulated Aggressiveness in Monkeys. *J. Nerv. Ment. Dis.,* 144: 383–90.

Milgram, S. 1968. Some Conditions of Obedience and Disobedience to Authority. *Internat. J. Psychiat.,* 6: 259–76.

SUGGESTIONS FOR FURTHER READING

Daniels, D. N., Gilula, M. F., and Ochberg, F. M., eds. 1970. *Violence and the Struggle for Existence.* Boston: Little, Brown & Co.

Frank, J. D. 1967. *Sanity and Survival: Psychological Aspects of War and Peace.* New York: Random House.

Fried, M., Harris, M., and Murphy, R., eds. 1968. *War: The Anthropology of Armed Conflict and Aggression.* Garden City, N.Y.: Natural History Press.

a. leon higginbotham, jr.

7

THE BLACK PRISONER:

AMERICA'S CAGED CANARY

Introduction: America's prisons and jails are a scandal. Most are physically and organizationally antiquated, financially starved, cruelly overcrowded, and corruption-ridden hell-holes of homosexuality and violence. They seem, however, to be fairly effective schools for

A. Leon Higginbotham is judge of the United States District Court for the Eastern District of Pennsylvania. A graduate of Antioch College and Yale Law School, he formerly served as assistant district attorney for Philadelphia County and as a commissioner of the Federal Trade Commission. He was appointed by Chief Justice Earl Warren to the Commission on Reform of Federal Criminal Laws, and he served as vice-chairman of the National Commission of the Causes and Prevention of Violence. A part of Judge Higginbotham's paper has previously appeared in *Outside Looking In*, A Series of Monographs Assessing the Effectiveness of Corrections (Washington, D.C.: Law Enforcement Assistance Administration, 1970).

criminal instruction. Why does the world's richest nation tolerate this? The primary reasons seem to be, first, that they lack a political constituency that in other bureaucracies generates pressure for increased support. Convicted felons are disfranchised, and tax-ridden voters are notoriously loath to increase their burden in the interest of prison reform.

Second, and more important, is the American public's hard line attitude. A Gallup poll in 1971 revealed that 75 percent of the adult population agreed that "convicted criminals are let off too easily." Worse, there are grave disagreements between whites and blacks about the effectiveness and fairness of our system of criminal justice. The same Gallup poll revealed that only 35 percent of blacks believe that American juries produce correct verdicts most of the time, compared with 53 percent of whites (in itself a frail majority). And some 70 percent of blacks believe that a Negro suspect is far more likely than a white one to be convicted and sentenced.

Leon Higginbotham, a black federal district judge in Philadelphia, sees the recent spate of prison riots as an ominous bellwether. Given our legacy of racism and violence, the riots indicate, he says, that we are in a "contest for urban and, in fact, national survival." On the resolution of this contest "the fate of our civilization may very well depend."

H. G. WELLS ONCE SAID, "Civilization is a race between education and catastrophe." Certainly our major cities are in an equally urgent race where present catastrophic trends have not been restrained with viable constructive solutions. The fate of our civilization may very well depend on whether the constructive forces can overtake the momentum of destruction. In this contest for urban and, in fact, national survival our capacity to understand the issues of racism and violence is essential.

I will not open my inquiry by quoting urbanologists, sociologists, city planners, politicians, criminologists, policemen, lawyers, or other purported experts on urban survival, but rather a poet. For poets often capture in a very few words the nub of the issue better than the thousands of words issued by presidential commissions, academicians, or activists. Here are Langston Hughes's thoughts as to what happens to "a dream deferred":

> What happens to a dream deferred?
> Does it dry up like a raisin in the sun
> Or fester like a sore and then run?
> Does it stink like rotten meat
> Or crust and sugar over like a syrupy sweet?
> Maybe it just sags like a heavy load
> Or does it explode?[1]

On the issues of racism and violence as they affect the black community, what will happen to this dream deferred? Will it sag like a heavy load or will it explode? For 345 years, from 1619 to 1964, America was generally free from any sustained violent confrontations—other than sporadic slave revolts—initiated by blacks in response to the general deferment of a dream. In fact, more often the dream in Langston Hughes's term "sagged like a heavy load" on the backs of 15 to 20 million black Americans. "Explosions" initiated by blacks have been infrequent and even then of a relatively minor magnitude. But will the first 345 years of precedent be followed for the next 3 years or the next 3 decades without explosions or without greater turmoil? To forecast the future and understand the present, we must appreciate the nature of time as a continuum. Daniel Bell, chairman of the Commission on the Year 2000, has written:

---

[1] From "Harlem," in *Selected Poems of Langston Hughes* (New York: Alfred A. Knopf, Inc., 1959); quoted by permission of the publisher.

Time, said St. Augustine, is a three-fold present: the present as we experience it, the past as a present memory, and the future as a present expectation. By that criterion, the world of the year 2000 has already arrived, for in the decisions we make now, in the way we design our environment and thus sketch the lines of constraints, the future is committed. . . . The future is not an overarching leap into the distance; it begins in the present.[2]

Similarly our present of the 1970s has been partially determined by our history of 30, 100, and 300 years ago.

In evaluating our present or forecasting the future as to the aspects of racism and violence in America, let us avoid clichés, slogans, or easy conclusions such as "law and order," "law, order, and justice," "power to the people," or "the rule of law." For far too long we have been victimized by supergeneralizations such as "the forgotten American," "the silent majority," "the radical liberal," "the solid conservative." Instead, let us start with a case study. Let us look at a specific urban event and ponder its present relevance and its historical antecedents.

Let us look at one event which took place on July 4, 1970, in Philadephia, Pennsylvania. Let us examine that event and inquire, how relevant was yesterday's racism in causing it? How relevant is yesterday's racism to today's escalating urban violence? Is there any relation between the good guys' failures, the law-abiding community's failure, to provide adequate resources and the subsequent riots? Does not this case study suggest that we will never be able to contain present urban criminal violence unless we have as an equal and major priority a commitment to contain racism, poverty, and injustice?

On July 4, 1970, Bob Hope, Billy Graham, and 350,000 persons celebrated Honor America Day in Washington, D.C.[3]

---

[2] Daniel Bell, "The Year 2000—the Trajectory of an Idea," *Daedulus,* 96 (Summer 1967): 639.

[3] Earlier that week, along with John Cardinal Krol and the managers of the Philadelphia Eagles football team and the Phillies baseball team, I had talked to Bob Hope in support of Honor America Day.

Throughout the nation, many were speaking about the "living spirit of the Fourth of July." Superstars gave their talents; thousands gave their prayers, songs, and cheers. For the Washington celebration, President Nixon said:

We look back today over almost 200 years to a group of men meeting in Philadelphia and we look back in pride and in wonder, for what they did on this day is the single greatest political achievement in the history of man. And we are the beneficiaries of that achievement. . . .

Yet, there is something remaining to be done in order to make Honor America Day the kind of special occasion we all want it to be. It is my hope that each of us will take away not only our proud memories of this day, but also the living spirit of the Fourth of July as well, a spirit that created a free and strong and prosperous nation.

That is the spirit that can truly honor America, not only today, but always.[4]

While Fourth of July orators were lauding the principles involved in our nation's first violent revolution, at Philadelphia a riot started at Holmesburg Prison. There was fighting between black and white prisoners, armed with knives, cleavers, and other instruments seized from the chief steward's office in the worst riot Holmesburg Prison had ever seen. About 400 of the 1,300 prisoners were involved in the disorder, which started about 1:10 P.M. in the mess hall, when a black prisoner punched a white guard, who fell to the floor. Police Commissioner Frank L. Rizzo reported that this immediately set whites and blacks at each other, guards became involved, and six were used as hostages. Some were beaten and at least one was stabbed before they were released when heavily armed police and dogs poured into the prison. Eighty-five percent of the 1,300 Holmesburg prisoners are black.

A week after the riot the superintendent of the prison reported that they had segregated the institution's white and black prisoners

[4] Recorded message of President Richard M. Nixon at the "Honor America Day" celebration in Washington, D.C., July 4, 1970, from *Weekly Compilation of Presidential Documents*, 6 (July 13, 1970): 892.

as a temporary emergency measure to help prevent further out-breaks of violence. In the riot more than eighty prisoners and twenty-five guards were injured. Superintendent Hendricks placed the blame on "hard-core black militants." The rioting was not totally racial. All of the black prisoners did not attack all of the whites. As Superintendent Hendricks reported, some black guards were stabbed by black inmates and many blacks came to the defense of whites. Yet no one can deny the heavy racial components of these incidents.

A report prepared by the Philadelphia district attorney starts with these excerpts:

They then took us out of the hallway and put us in the bread room and threatened to kill us. We were there about two hours until the police guards came in. I was holding a man's hand on for him because it was chopped off with a meat cleaver.

W. G., INMATE

I saw a guard standing outside the mess hall. He was bleeding around the left side of neck and chest. . . . guys ran in and picked up knives and sticks. I don't know who they were. I went into the kitchen and got something to eat. I sat in the kitchen and ate some chicken salad.

R. M., INMATE

That is when I seen Rat and another inmate known as Shotgun stabbing white inmates. Rat said, "any of you niggers who is not with us, is going to die like the whites." He proceeded to stab another white. Then we started to run out, and the water hose was on, and Rat was running up and down with a knife in his hand, shouting, "kill the whites."

K. S., INMATE

I was then alone with the inmates and the riot doors were closed and locked, trapping me inside. . . . I was told by one of the inmates to put on a prison shirt that was lying on the floor in front of the laundry. I put the shirt on and someone gave me a bag to wear, like an apron, to hide my guard's uniform.

H. C., GUARD

So we managed to make it to the back of the mess hall and hid under the back table. They then started grabbing us three at a time. They were yelling "three at a time, three at a time," chopping them up with meat cleavers. They were chopping them up. The last three that they took, they picked a kid who was on top of me and a couple more, making three, and they took them out, stabbing them, chopping them. So I started to pray.

J. B., INMATE

I became particularly interested in this riot because the transcript of the official police radio tapes reads as follows:

2:40 P.M. C-3, The inmates say they will talk to Judge Higginbotham, and will surrender to him. They say they will listen to him.

2:47 P.M. C-3, We have 3 badly bleeding hospital cases, the fire dept. is going to try to remove an iron grate, and try to get them out. Car #1 notified information from the mayor, Judge Higginbotham is at Ocean City, N.J. C-3. Try to get a helicopter to go down to get him.[5]

I began with a description of an urban prison riot because prisoners may be symbolically the caged canaries of our societies. Why do I use the term caged canary? Because decades ago, men entered the mines with caged canaries on their hats. Since the canary was less strong than the miner, it would be the first to become ill and thus indicate that there was a high level of toxicity or pollution which would endanger the miners' lives. As I look at the events, the outcries, the rage, and the rioting at many prisons, I see hundreds of caged canaries warning us that our urban society is in serious danger, that our very survival is threatened.

Yet warning signals are not enough, for we have received warning signals before of malignant pathology or extraordinary dangers. Approximately two decades ago, while the activists in the civilian population were integrating lunch counters and depart-

[5] Even though the police sent officials attempting to find me in Ocean City, they could not locate me since I was playing in an amateur tennis tournament.

ment stores throughout the South, a relatively "impotent" movement was garnering support. Hundreds of prisoners were becoming interested in what some thought was an irrelevant and weird faith —the Black Muslims. The Kerner Commission noted:

A major factor intensifying the civil rights movement was widespread Negro unemployment and poverty; an important force in awakening Negro protest was the meteoric rise to national prominence of the Black Muslims, established around 1930. The organization reached the peak of its influence when more progress toward equal rights was being made than ever before in American history while at the same time economic opportunity for the poorest groups in the urban ghettos was stagnating.

Increasing unemployment among Negroes, combined with the revolution in expectations, created a climate in which the Black Muslims thrived. They preached a vision of the doom of the white "devils" and the coming dominance of the black man, promised a utopian paradise of a separate territory within the United States for a Negro state, and offered a practical program of building Negro business through hard work, thrift, and racial unity. To those willing to submit to the rigid discipline of the movement, the Black Muslims organization gave a sense of purpose and dignity.[6]

Malcolm X was paroled from prison in 1951, and he writes of his experiences in the early 1960s: "I have lectured in Negro colleges and some of these brainwashed black Ph.D's, with their suspenders dragging the ground with degrees, have run to the white man's newspaper calling me a 'black fanatic.' "[7] Yet, while Malcolm X was supposedly a black fanatic in the early 1960s, thought by many to be unimportant and ineffective, now in 1970, after his death, several schools bear his name. *The Autobiography of Malcolm X* is one of the most popular books at predominantly black colleges and is widely read by thoughtful persons of all ages.

Thus maybe an analysis of the Philadelphia July 4 prison riot (or the hundreds of others like it which have occurred in the last

---

[6] *Report of the National Advisory Commission on Civil Disorders,* New York Times edition (New York: E. P. Dutton & Co., 1968), p. 229.

[7] *The Autobiography of Malcolm X* (New York: Grove Press, 1966), p. 181.

decade) can alert us as to how violent the future of our cities could be if prisoners, by their conduct, are providing warning signals for the whole urban society. Are prisoners by their seemingly pathological reaction indicating the degree of black-versus-white rage existing in many urban communities? For, if within the security of prisons one is not able to assure personal safety, does it suggest that we may not be able to assure personal safety in our urban communities if we keep on doing business as usual and if we fail to eliminate the causes of hatred, polarization, and despair? Do these riots give us a message as to what could be the nature of our society five years, ten years, or twenty years hence?

To the bigot, the ignorant, or the unsophisticated, the Philadelphia riot is explainable in simplistic terms. They would suggest that this riot was just another example of expanding "black crime" and the need for tougher law enforcement. For the scholar and the thoughtful, however, the issue has greater complexity. It requires one to ask, what were the immediate and long-term causes? Does "black crime" have any relationship with past "white injustices?"

Though the Philadelphia Prison riot does indicate how acute some of the tensions are when at their most distorted levels, I would be the first to emphasize that as a case study it is not a fully representative sample, or even a balanced example or spectrum, of the present tensions in our society. This is so because it exemplifies only a confrontation of blacks against whites, and the data of the Violence Commission demonstrate clearly that except for robbery most of the victims of violent crimes in the cities are blacks who have been assaulted by blacks.

The commission found:

There is a widespread public misconception that most violent crime is committed by black offenders against white victims. This is not true. Our Task Force Victim-Offender Survey covering seventeen cities has confirmed other evidence that serious assaultive violence in the city—homicide, aggravated assault and rape—is predominantly between white offenders and white victims and black offenders and black victims. The majority of these crimes involves blacks attacking blacks, while most of the remainder involve whites victimizing whites. Indeed, our Survey found that 90 percent of urban homicide, aggravated assaults and rapes involve victims and offenders of the same race.

In two-thirds of homicides and aggravated assaults in the city, and in three-fifths of the rapes, the victim is a Negro.[8]

But even though the Phildelphia prison riot is not a representative case study, it is nevertheless relevant because it was (1) a riot in an urban prison; (2) the inmates had been arrested for crimes purportedly committed in a city; (3) 85 percent of the inmates were black; and (4) most important, the conditions in the prison reflected decades of community neglect and persistent failures to provide adequate resources for our correctional and criminal justice system. The district attorney, Arlen Specter, noted:

Nor is it possible to discount the fact that there was a strong racial element in the riot . . . but to attempt to explain the riot purely as a racial conflict equally disregards a number of salient facts. . . . No one familiar with the riot situation on July 4th can doubt that black rage played a major part. Nor should this be surprising. Racial antagonism is still far too prevelant in American society as a whole, and this antagonism is heightened by the frustration of prison life, the obvious fact that blacks make up 85 percent of the prison population at Holmesburg, the preaching of race hatred by militant groups . . . groups whose members make up a disproportionate percentage of the rioters. . . . The events equally prove that only a small minority of any race— even among accused prisoners who are at odds with society . . . is willing to take the path of violence. . . . Not only is the prison overcrowded to twice its capacity, destroying even the minimum privacy which prison life can afford, but the cells are aging, dingy and in many cases windowless. But it is not the physical condition, the presence of roaches or the institutional cooking which contributed most to the frustrations of the prisoners . . . nor is there complaint of guard brutality preceding the riot.

The district attorney concluded his recommendation:

The July 4, 1970, riot clearly represented a failure of the entire system of criminal justice in Philadelphia which was only reflected in the last instance by a collapse in the prisons. For, so long as it is in the

[8] *To Establish Justice, To Insure Domestic Tranquility*, Final Report of the National Commission on the Causes and Prevention of Violence (Washington, D.C.: Government Printing Office, 1969), p. 24.

interests of defense attorneys to seek trial delay, so long as only in-adequate numbers of defense attorneys are available to represent in-digent defendants, so long as too few assistant district attorneys are available to prosecute cases and too few judges, support personnel, and courtrooms are available for trial of these cases, so long as all of the participants in the criminal justice system are discouraged by the apparently insurmountable problems of guaranteeing fair and speedy trials for all those accused and equally prompt and fair sentencing for those convicted, no one can be surprised at the frustration and aliena-tion of prisoners who have already shown their disaffection with society by the acts which brought them to prison in the first place. Thus, any aim at solution must involve the entire system of criminal justice.

While I do not disagree with the district attorney's analysis that the events at the Philadelphia prison were caused by failures in the entire system of criminal justice, let us examine a period which preceded the breakdown of the criminal justice system.

Numerous other studies, including the fifteen volumes of reports to the Violence Commission, warn us of the impending doom of our cities by their citation of thousands of pages of data. Yet in this analysis I have focused on one prison riot because it sym-bolizes a more basic issue than just another riot. It dramatizes the issue of the relationship between the riot of July 4, 1970, and our nation's failure in Philadelphia on July 4, 1776.

Perhaps the riot asks us: Can we have long-term racial peace or justice within correctional institutions without a determined com-mitment to obliterate racism in our society generally? Perhaps the riots pose for each one of us the question: have we personally contributed to prison rioting by sanctioning overt racism or by re-maining a part of a silent majority, which fails to condemn racism or fails actively to work towards its eradication? Perhaps the riot begs us to look honestly at our nation's true racial heritage and to put today's problems in a fair and honest racial historical perspec-tive. Perhaps the rioting requires us to answer the question of why it is that so many men have become, in the words of Super-intendent Hendricks, "hard core black militants."

Many public officials are not willing to talk with candor on the public record about racism, past and present, in our society. To this vacuum of inattention I direct my remarks. To some extent I may annoy many. For there are bitter racial truths of the past which many would like to forget. And there are difficult problems of the present which may seem almost unsolvable. But we do not aid the cause of justice by acting as if these problems are non-existent or can be solved merely by waiting until tomorrow.

Perhaps we can gain some insights from the story about the New England judge who presided over a suburban juvenile court. Above his chair in his mahogany-paneled courtroom was a huge picture of George Washington. In making inquiries to ascertain whether a particular juvenile was fit for probation, the judge would ask two questions. The first question was, "Who is the man in back of me?" If the boy responded, "George Washington," the judge thought that the juvenile had sufficient intellectual acumen to perhaps be amenable to the process of reasoning. Then he would ask the juvenile, "What was George Washington most famous for?" If the juvenile instinctively replied, "He never told a lie," the judge felt that the juvenile had then demonstrated sufficient moral character to be deemed worthy of probation.

Finally, one day, a black lad charged with delinquency came before the New England judge. As some of you may know, in the urban centers and in the suburban centers black and white are not always in perfect communication, and the black boy had not learned the judge's interrogation game, which all of the white boys knew. To the first question asked the black boy instantly replied, "George Washington." To the second question, "What is that man most famous for?" the young black boy hesitated. He looked at the floor, then he looked up at the ceiling. The judge repeated his question, "What is that man most famous for?" Then, without batting an eye, the boy looked directly at the judge and said, "Sir, he is most famous for owning slaves." And thus, in the two different responses you have capsuled the issue of law, order, and racism.

I submit that there is an interrelationship between our failures on July 4, 1776 and what happens in prison racial riots in 1970. Let us start out by honestly facing the issue of what was the nature and breadth of our democracy during those good old days of our forefathers. There has always been a fundamental ambiguity in the collective commitment of this society to the ideals upon which it is allegedly based. From a racial historical perspective, the most often quoted words of the Declaration of Independence, "We hold these truths to be self-evident, that all men are created equal," were in fact at the very hour of their declaration being repudiated by the racial practices in this nation. For the perspective of my present remarks, perhaps the most relevant words in the Declaration of Independence would be the statement that "The History of the present King of Great-Britain is a History of repeated Injuries and Usurpations, all having in direct Object the Establishment of an absolute Tyranny over the States. *To prove this, let Facts be submitted to a candid World"* (italics added). Thus, in the words of the Declaration of Independence, can America be receptive to having *facts submitted candidly* within a historic racial perspective, facts which speak not of the king's tyranny over states but of our forefather's tyranny over black men? We should welcome my candor if we truly desire to get optimum racial peace in our correctional institutions and in our society generally.

In 1775, the Continental Congress met in Philadelphia and noted its declaration of the causes and the necessity of taking up arms, stating that: "Our cause is just . . . Our internal resources are great. . . . the arms we have been compelled by our enemies to assume, we will, in defiance of every hazard . . . employ for the preservation of liberties; being with one mind *resolved to die free men rather than to live slaves"* (italics added). While the founding fathers did not want to be slaves of the king, they nevertheless repudiated freedom for black men.

As Thomas Jefferson was to observe later, his draft of July 2 included a clause "reprobating the enslaving the inhabitants of

Africa, [which] was struck out in [deference] to South Carolina and Georgia, who had never attempted to restrain the importation of slaves and who on the contrary still wished to continue it."

Not only is there a correlation between the problems we now face because of the failures of our founding fathers to take a forthright position in 1776, we must also recognize that from its very origin in 1787, our Constitution was in part a racist document. For at least seventy-eight years through the full force of law it sanctioned racism and its devastating brutality. The law and order of that day, the Preamble of the Constitution, states:

We the People of the United States, in Order to form a more perfect Union, establish Justice, insure domestic Tranquility, provide for the common defence, promote the general Welfare, and secure the Blessings of Liberty to ourselves and our Posterity, do ordain and establish this Constitution for the United States of America.

Yet that did not mean a perfect union for blacks. It did not mean justice for blacks, it did not mean promoting the general welfare for blacks, it did not mean the blessings of liberty for blacks, and it was unconcerned about their posterity.

Article I, section 2 of the Constitution provided at that time that:

Representatives and direct Taxes shall be apportioned among the several States . . . according to their respective Numbers, which shall be determined by adding to the whole Number of free Persons, including those bound to Service for a Term of Years, and excluding Indians not taxed, three-fifths of all other Persons.

This section was so artfully drawn that it demonstrated at that first constitutional convention what I believe is true now and has been true ever since that date—the greater political skills of the southern legislators. For in that document, when using the term "three-fifths of all other persons," they studiously avoided the word "slaves" and thus avoided making manifest on its face that it was a document which sanctioned cruelty to mankind. What article I, section 2 really meant was that a southern planter owning 500 slaves would, when electing representatives for the United

States Congress, have 300 times greater leverage than one businessman or a free citizen of Massachusetts.

When the issue of ratification of the Constitution was before the South Carolina House of Representatives one of the framers of the Constitution, General Charles Cotesworth Pinckney, spoke to that body on the issue of slavery. He said:

> I am of the same opinion now as I was two years ago, when I used the expressions the gentleman has quoted . . . that while there remained one acre of swamp land uncleared of South Carolina, I would raise my voice against restricting the importation of Negroes. I am as thoroughly convinced as that gentleman is, that the nature of our climate and the flat, swampy situation of our country, obliges us to cultivate our lands with Negroes, and without them South Carolina would soon be a desert waste.

Some of you may ask, what is the relevance of the ratification of the United States Constitution in 1789 to today's correctional problems? What is the relevance of General Pinckney's 1789 remarks to riots in the 1970s? For such relevance I suggest again that you read Malcolm X's description of his experiences in prison and his talks with Black Muslims there. Think first in terms of what General Pinckney said, and then listen to Malcolm X's reaction to the importation of Negroes. He describes his early conversations with a follower of the Honorable Elijah Muhammad in prison, where the follower said to Malcolm: "You don't even know who you are . . . You don't even know, the white devil has hidden it from you, that you are of a race of people of ancient civilizations and riches in gold and kings. You don't even know your true family name, you wouldn't recognize your true language if you heard it. You've been cut off by the devil white man from all true knowledge of your own kind. You have been a victim of the evil of the devil white man ever since he murdered and raped and stole you from your native land in the seeds of your forefathers. . . ."[9] Malcolm X describes his beliefs as they became

[9] *The Autobiography of Malcolm X*, p. 161.

developed in prison, as he became a believer in the Honorable Elijah Muhammad. From his studying, he concluded:

Human history's greatest crime was the traffic in black flesh when the devil white man went into Africa and murdered and kidnapped to bring to the West in chains, in slave ships, millions of black men, women, and children, who were worked and beaten and tortured as slaves.

The devil white man cut these black people off from all knowledge of their own kind, and cut them off from any knowledge of their own language, religion, and past culture, until the black man in America was the earth's only race of people who had absolutely no knowledge of his true identity.

In one generation, the black slave women in America had been raped by the slavemaster white man until there had begun to emerge a homemade, handmade, brainwashed race that was no longer even of its true color, that no longer even knew its true family names. The slavemasters forced his family name upon this rape-mixed race, which the slavemaster began to call "the Negro."[10]

Why have I taken time out to cite our nation's constitutional heritage and to compare it with Malcolm X's comment? Is it to antagonize you, to anger you? Of course not! I cite this history because we will never be able to communicate to thousands of black men locked up in our prisons today unless we at first honestly look at our past history. We will not be able to solve today's racial problems either in our prisons or on the outside merely by suggesting that some of the black men who are angry are a few isolated hard core militants. Perhaps we make the first step of the long hard journey ahead by our honesty and willingness to admit that our nation has caused much rage, that our nation has often been grossly unjust in the treatment of blacks, and that we have an obligation to work swiftly to eradicate the many consequences of that injustice rather than to keep pretending that the problem never existed.

In his famous opinion in the Dred Scott case, Chief Justice

---

[10] *Ibid.*, p. 162.

Roger B. Taney, writing for the Supreme Court, held in 1857 that a black man

had no rights which the white man was bound to respect; and that the negro might justly and lawfully be reduced to slavery for his benefit. He was bought and sold, and treated as an ordinary article of merchandise and traffic, whenever a profit could be made by it. This opinion was at that time fixed and universal in the civilized portion of the white race. It was regarded as an axiom in morals as well as in politics, which no one thought of disputing, or supposed to be open to dispute; and men in every grade and position in society daily and habitually acted upon it in their private pursuits, as well as in matters of public concern, without doubting for a moment the correctness of this opinion.

Again, that was law and order as pronounced by the Supreme Court. When in 1896 Mr. Justice Brown's opinion in *Plessy* v. *Ferguson* sanctioned state-imposed racial segregation, that also represented a concept of law and order, one which retarded our nation for more than five decades and whose tragic aftermath we are still witnessing and suffering from today. As thousands of laws have been ground out and reinforced by new governmental and business practices, we have often had law and order, but not racial justice. The reader is entitled to an evaluation beyond 1776 and beyond 1896. So let us look at the issue of racism during the last thirty years, and particularly since the termination of World War II, presumably fought for the four freedoms. During this thirty-year period, of course, there have been significant steps towards repudiating the old racial injustice: the United States Supreme Court's opinions in 1944 in *Smith* v. *Allwright*, the key primary voting rights case; *Brown* v. *Board of Education* in 1954; the several civil rights acts from the late 1950s to the Fair Housing Act of 1968; the proliferation of executive orders and fair housing laws and fair employment laws. All of these constituted advances toward creating law and order within a context of justice. Yet is it these advances which advocates of law and order are urging and supporting? Or are they talking about a concept of law and order which merely keeps the lid on riots, without any concern about the economic and racial causes of rioting, without any concern about eliminating rat-filled homes and overcrowded schools, and without concern about opening the doors to employment opportunities?

So that no one will misunderstand me, I am concerned about the outbreak of riots and massive public disorders. I do not urge, I do not sanction, I do not suggest violence as a way to correct our system. And I appreciate that law enforcement officials are obligated to use reasonable force to bring these outbreaks to an end at the earliest possible time. Yet I am concerned equally about these individuals who condemn only the riots without any willingness to probe the causes.

I have been discussing the linkage between our past racist practices and today's racial tensions. But the task of the professional, the social scientist, the educated man, and the concerned citizen is far greater than that of being merely an issue raiser. In a real sense, he must have the capacity to be an issue resolver. So where do we go from here? We may have a full awareness that law and order has not always been synonymous with justice when it comes to the black man. Can we have justice in this decade in our nation? The Kerner Commission—the 1968 National Advisory Commission on Civil Disorders—in talking about racial division, said:

This deepening racial division is not inevitable. The movement apart can be reversed. Choice is still possible. Our principal task is to define that choice and to press for a national resolution.

To pursue our present course will involve the continuing polarization of the American community and, ultimately, the destruction of basic democratic values.

The alternative is not blind repression or capitulation to lawlessness. It is the realization of common opportunities for all within a single society.

This alternative will require a commitment to national action—compassionate, massive and sustained, backed by the resources of the most powerful and the richest nation on this earth. From every American it will require new attitudes, new understanding, and, above all, new will.

The vital needs of the nation must be met; hard choices must be made, and, if necessary, new taxes enacted.[11]

This commission, composed of eleven moderate Americans of whom only two were black, said in its introduction: "What white Americans have never fully understood—but what the Negro can never forget—is that white society is deeply implicated in the ghetto, white institutions created it, white institutions maintain it, and white society condones it."

I submit that any objective scholarly study would corroborate the Kerner Commission's conclusions. And more important, a major factor in every prison racial riot is that most black prisoners believe, as the Kerner Commission found, that "white society is deeply implicated in the ghetto, white institutions created it, white institutions maintain it, and white society condones it."

In recent years there have been massive appeals to the person who is described as the "forgotten American." The forgotten American is purported to be one who does not walk in picket lines, does not join protest organizations, pays his taxes, and seldom complains about his country. Certainly I appreciate this forgotten American's patriotism and love for his country and I applaud him for it. But I wonder whether the mythical forgotten American could more aptly be described as a "forgetting American," one who has made it and is willing to forget about the lack of justice and opportunity for those on the other side of the track and in the ghetto. As I view my college generation, it was predominantly a silent generation, which later rose into the affluent society and invaded suburbia. Now many of these illustrious graduates, after having made it, believe that they are the forgotten Americans. But they have won the major benefits from our society. It was not necessary for them to picket to get a hot dog in a five-and-ten-cent store in Birmingham, nor to petition the Presi-

[11] *Report of the National Advisory Commission on Civil Disorders,* pp. 1–2.

dent to guarantee their southern relatives the right to vote in Mississippi or Alabama or Georgia; they needed no executive order to bar their employer from racial or religious discrimination. Thus, if we really are going to meet the question, if we are going to solve the problem of law, order, and justice, we have got to talk in terms of massive programs for employment, education, welfare, housing, health; substantial improvement in the functioning of law enforcement agencies, our courts, and what in so many states is the sad, sad, almost medieval quality of our penology and correctional systems. This is the challenge for the educated man, this is the challenge for these scientists, to move past the simplicity of the catch-phrase slogan of law and order and to create the system, the mechanism of a new tomorrow which assures to all of our citizens a concept of law and order which is truly based on "justice for all."

The problems of violence in the urban or black communities cannot be solved by the massive collection of black crime data or simplistic rhetoric which does not probe the causes of crime. Our entire society is crushed by these increasing disparities in crime rates, and blacks suffer most, for they are the most frequent victims of physical violence in the urban community. We must recognize that far more significant than statistical compilations of yesterday's crime rates is the reality of the relationship between our forefathers' failures on July 4, 1776, all of the subsequent intermittent failures throughout the years, and the prison racial riots and present black rage of the 1970s. The issue is not whether we should condemn our forefathers for their failures or even our generation for our failures. But instead the issue is whether we can now move forward together and agree to spend the billions of dollars which are needed to eradicate the pathology of racism and its attendant failures in housing, employment, health care, education, and the maladministration of justice.

Of course we must make full and immediate improvements in correcting our failures in the criminal justice system and particularly our failures in the correctional system and in the processing of criminal cases. I make a plea not solely for black Americans. I make a plea that this nation demonstrate its resolve to eliminate the total pathology of poverty, the total pathology of injustice. We must give all of the victims, whether they are white or black, brown or yellow, from North or South, East or West, a new opportunity for full dignity in the development of their maximum potential. Too many persons feel that they can do nothing to influence the direction and destiny of this nation. Too many persons blame the tragedies of the hour on some purported hard core black militants, student agitators, or nondescript outsiders.

Because of our refusal to solve the real, critical problems, because of our persistent preference to scream the easy cliché as a substitute for action, I sometimes wonder whether our nation will be able to reach its potential of greatness. In fact, I sometimes wonder about our long-term capacity for survival. I wonder whether we will take those necessary steps to deescalate either prison racial tensions or the nation's racial tensions. The Violence Commission concluded its introduction by saying:

When in man's long history other great civilizations fell, it was less often from external assault than from internal decay. Our own civilization has shown a remarkable capacity for responding to crises and for emerging to higher pinnacles of power and achievement. But our most serious challenges to date have been external—the kind this strong and resourceful country could unite against. While serious external dangers remain, the graver threats today are internal: haphazard urbanization, racial discrimination, disfiguring of the environment, unprecedented interdependence, the dislocation of human identity and motivation created by an affluent society—all resulting in a rising tide of individual and group violence.

The greatness and durability of most civilizations has been finally determined by how they have responded to these challenges from within. Ours will be no exception.[12]

In my separate statement with the Violence Commission I quoted a distinguished black psychiatrist, Dr. Price Cobb, who

---

[12] *To Establish Justice, To Insure Domestic Tranquility*, p. xxxii.

expressed a concern which is even more urgent now than when it was uttered a year ago:

If violence continues at its present pace, we may well witness the end of the grand experiment of democracy. The unheeded report of the Kerner Commission pinpointed the cause of our urban violence, and this report presents the tragic consequences when those in power fail to act on behalf of the weak as well as the powerful.

This country can no longer tolerate the divisions of black and white, haves and have-nots. The pace of events has quickened and dissatisfactions no longer wait for a remedy.

There are fewer great men among us to counsel patience. Their voices have been stilled by the very violence they sought to prevent. Martin Luther King, Jr., the noble advocate of nonviolence, may have been the last great voice warning the country to cancel its rendezvous with violence before it is too late.

The truth is plain to see. If the racial situation remains inflammatory and the conditions perpetuating poverty remain unchanged, and if vast numbers of our young see small hope for improvement in the quality of their lives, then this country will remain in danger. Violence will not go away because we will it and any superficial whitewash will sooner or later be recognized.[13]

Let me conclude, as I started, by quoting the same great black poet, Langston Hughes. In "A Dream Deferred" he reminded us that the deferment may cause it some day to explode, and at a later date he wrote a poem—"Dream of Freedom"—where he said:

There is a dream in the land
With its back against the wall.
By muddled names and strange
Sometimes the dream is called.

There are those who claim
This dream for theirs alone—
A sin for which, we know,
They must atone.

Unless shared in common
Like sunlight and like air,
The dream will die for lack
Of substance anywhere.

[13] *Ibid.*, pp. ix-x.

The dream knows no frontier or tongue,
The dream no class or race
The dream cannot be kept secure
In any one locked place.

This dream today embattled,
With its back against the wall—
To save the dream for one
It must be saved for all.[14]

If we want more personal safety in the urban community, if we want a decrease of polarization and a decrease of hatred and hopelessness, let us start out with an unequivocal recognition that radical improvements are required and "To save this dream for one, It must be saved for all."

[14] "Dream of Freedom," delivered at the commencement exercises of Wayne State University, July 1964. Reprinted by permission of Harold Ober Associates Incorporated. Copyright © 1964 by Langston Hughes.

david brinkley

8

THE ESTABLISHMENT

AND THE REVOLUTIONARIES

Introduction: David Brinkley is unhappy with both the revolutionaries and the establishment. Curiously, these two most discordant groups seem to enjoy a kind of inverse symbiotic relationship in contemporary America: the revolutionaries feed off the rigidities and blunders of the establishment, while the latter's bureaucratic

David Brinkley has reported the news on radio and television for the National Broadcasting Company since 1943. A native of Wilmington, North Carolina and a student at both the University of North Carolina and Vanderbilt University, he worked as a reporter for the Wilmington *Star-News* from 1938 to 1940, as an army infantryman from 1940 to 1942, then as a United Press reporter until he joined NBC in 1943. In 1956 he first teamed with Chet Huntley in covering the Democratic National Convention at Chicago. Since then the Huntley-Brinkley Report has won every major broadcasting award.

conservatism is bolstered because its more radical assailants are so widely unpopular. Brinkley uses the terms revolutionary and radical interchangeably and he nowhere defines what a radical is or explains whether radicals, presumably of the left, are necessarily violent revolutionaries. Many contemporary radicals who realistically share Brinkley's assessment of the heavy public odds against them claim to seek a "psycho-cultural" rather than a political and violent revolution. But the American public is impatient with fine distinctions, and its massive disgust for what it broadly perceives as radical behavior has apparently been growing during the past three decades—to the considerable alarm of civil libertarians. According to the public opinion polls, the *maximum* percentage of Americans approving free speech for "extremists" during the 1940s peaked at 49 percent. In the 1950s it never reached beyond 29 percent, and in the turbulent 1960s it reached a new low of only 21 percent. Shortly after the bloody confrontations between protesters and police at the August, 1968, Democratic Convention—an affray in which the mass media generally regarded the protesters with some sympathy and which the Violence Commission's "Walker Report" bluntly labeled a "police riot"—the Survey Research Center reported that only 19 percent of its nationwide sample of interviewees agreed that the Chicago police had used "too much force." A plurality of 32 percent responded that the police had used the "right amount" of force, and an additional 25 percent insisted that "not enough" police force had been employed. Put another way, a solid majority of 57 percent either approved the "police riot" or regarded it as too timid!

In light of this apparently growing surly mood, Brinkley's contention that "if, indeed, we have a violent confrontation, the radical *left* will be its object and its victim" seems altogether probable. That such a respected national broadcaster should contend that if our social structure is destroyed by violence, "what will appear will be martial law, a military dictatorship, and a police state" is sobering testimony to the disrepair of our national confidence. But he makes clear that the establishment, and especially the federal government, is far from blameless, for its swelling bureaucracies, with their insatiable appetites increasingly dwarfing their performance, have largely confirmed Max Weber's classic dictum that bureaucracies tend quickly to relegate their established purpose to secondary status and to concentrate their first efforts on the defense and enhancement of their empire. Brinkley's two concluding suggestions are both novel and constructive—although the first, which involves tax-refusal, invites further confrontation, and the second, which involves a kind of plebiscitory democracy, rests upon a public that has shown alarmingly little regard for those crucial First Amendment freedoms that have been the bedrock of our democracy.

REGRETTABLY, IT IS NOT NEWS that the stability of our country is threatened by violence—on campuses, in the big cities, in gunfights with the police, in arson and bombing. If this continues, society certainly will find a way to stop it—by legal means if possible, but by other means if necessary. These other means will be as harsh and repressive as they need to be, if not a little more so. If some of our constitutional and legal niceties get lost in this process, then it will be seen as regrettable but necessary.

Most of the American people, in talking to politicians and journalists and poll takers, are reluctant to use the word revolution because its connotations are almost too frightening to contemplate. But the word is widely used because it is widely thought that the basis for an attempted revolution is beginning to appear. And it is frequently said that what happens in the next few years will decide if an attempt at revolution actually occurs.

I do not believe any of that. Much of it I believe to be excited nonsense—nothing more than inflamed rhetoric. If we can learn anything from history, it is that a successful revolution, one that succeeds in overturning the established order and installing another one, must have the support of such institutions as the military, the working class and/or the middle class, and, at certain periods in history, the church. Yet those now advocating revolution in this country do not enjoy the support of any of these institutions— in fact, they enjoy the active hostility of all of them. This is why I say talk of a classic revolution in the United States is romantic or ignorant nonsense.

That is not to say that there is no possibility of a violent confrontation between the moderate and radical elements in American society. I believe that this is, in fact, more than a slight possibility. But if we have a violent confrontation, the radical *left* will be its object and its victim. It is so clearly outnumbered and outmanned and outgunned that it will lose, and lose quickly, almost without a contest.

So, in my view, there is no real possibility of a successful revolution overturning by violence the established order in this country. The means simply are not there. Presumably any attempt at revolution would be made because a sizable number of people, students and others, would have become so intensely dissatisfied with the structure of American society, so despairing of peaceful change, that they would try to force change by violence. Through human history a widely shared sense of popular grievance has most often been the cause of public violence—numerous people believing themselves to be oppressed, exploited, misgoverned, cheated, and lied to. In the French Revolution, and to some extent in the American Revolution, large groups of people believed that they were being abused by a selfish and arrogant royalty. But we also know that there are other causes of violence, not all of them so noble.

Violence can be a reaction against threats to comforts and privileges. Laboratory animals in cages will remain peaceful when there are not too many of them in a given space, when each is comfortable and well fed, and when the relationships between males and females are proceeding normally. But when the number of animals in a cage is increased radically, when overcrowding is severe, when their relationships with each other are disturbed, then the occupants of the cage become manic and violent.

Violence can also be a product of the aggressiveness that seems to be a part of the human personality. Usually we turn our aggressiveness into the form of wars. We clothe our aggressiveness in uniforms, supply it with bands and flags and guns. The next step then is to find a war, or create a war, to put our organized aggressiveness to use and call it patriotism.

And violence can be the product of boredom, the simple problem of having energy and nothing to do with it, the irritability and restlessness that come over all of us at times. And there is still another cause for violence, perhaps the most ignoble of all: the seeking of peer group approval.

One peer group we know about these days is the street gang, whose members feel some close relationship to each other and a hostility to everyone else. There are street gangs we know of— one in Chicago, for example—that will not accept a new member until he has committed a murder or until he has committed a robbery and has brought the money to the gang. And we know that there are small groups of radicals on numerous campuses who loathe and detest everything in American society except each other. In a group like that, one who blew up a university science lab would be a hero, a leader, a member of the group, and an important one, who had earned the respect of the men and the affections of the women. So when we talk of violence in America and when its defenders defend it, it is necessary to distinguish between violence with a nobility of purpose, as in the French and

American revolutions, and violence whose purposes are base, selfish, and stupid.

One of the stupidest and most ignorant ideas heard in modern times is the argument heard from radicals on campuses and elsewhere that this country is so terrible and so sick that the only cure is to kill it. In Vietnam some months ago, after the Air Force had obliterated a native village and killed just about everyone in it, an officer on the scene said, "We had to destroy it to save it." Well, that was insanity in Vietnam, and it is insanity in the United States. It is incredible to see those who hate the insanity in Vietnam express their hatred by introducing the same insanity here.

If the fabric of American society is torn apart by bombing and shooting and generalized violence—if anyone does not know what will appear in its place, I can tell him. There are not many things I think I know absolutely, but this I do know. What will appear will be martial law, a military dictatorship, and a police state. If the Weathermen and the Jerry Rubins and the Abbie Hoffmans and their friends who say they want to destroy the establishment, are able to do so, then when the police state appears, who will be arrested first? The question hardly needs an answer—the Weathermen and the Jerry Rubins and the Abbie Hoffmans and the rest. And the trial that they will get, if they get any trial at all, will make the trial of the Chicago Seven look like a picnic in the park.

Let us assume, for the sake of discussion, that those who blew up the science building at the University of Wisconsin and those who have burned and bombed other buildings on campus and off in numerous places have acted out of what they thought to be noble motives. As opposed to the other causes of violence, none of them noble in the least, let us assume that these acts were committed as honest acts of protest against an oppressive establishment.

We must admit first that many of the complaints against the American establishment are well justified—the establishment being, as I understand the term, persons and institutions in positions of leadership and policy making. As I understand it, to be a member of the establishment requires the exercise of some degree of power. So then we would have to include in this the federal government and local governments, the labor unions, the big corporations, the colleges and universities and foundations, the big communications media, and a few others. There isn't time here now to catalog all the sins of every group in that list, but we all know that they are numerous.

Let us consider only the most obvious one and the most powerful one: the federal government. A few of its leaders have dragged the American people into a brutal, destructive, and costly war without our consent, without even asking us—ramming it down our throats year after year against our clearly stated opposition, squandering our young men's lives to no purpose, squandering our money, raising taxes, inflating the economy, wasting our resources, killing the native population by the hundreds of thousands, destroying their country while seriously damaging ours, and all the while handing us one lie after another.

Our most powerful establishment institution, the federal government, does not serve our needs—it serves its own. Instead of producing the changes we obviously need it resists, because in the process it might lose some power and money. It never asks the people anything. It always tells us. It never asks what we want. It tells us what we're going to get. Then it tells us how much we have to pay for it. It tells us that we have to pay it or go to jail. And we usually wind up paying an extremely high price for something we didn't want in the first place and which most likely doesn't work anyway. The sociologist Max Weber pointed out a long time ago that a big bureaucracy, once established, ceases to work on the job it was given to do and begins working for itself, putting its best effort not into doing its job but into lobbying for more money, more staff, more power. In Washington, we see that principle at work every day. We see a massive array of bureaucrats interfering more and more in our private lives, taking our money away from us in the most arrogant and unfair ways, and then wasting most of it—always writing orders, announcing new regulations, and giving the answers to questions nobody ever asked.

If you doubt this, I invite you to try to think of one thing the federal bureaucracy does efficiently, fairly, and effectively. I think you will find it difficult. After twenty-five years of watching the federal bureaucracy at work, the only agencies I can think of that do their jobs effectively and fairly are a few small ones, including the Fish and Wildlife Service, the Park Service, the Forest Service, and perhaps the space agency. It is interesting to note that these agencies deal with fish, flowers, fields, forests, and the moon. They do not deal with the ordinary, everyday problems of the American people. This part of the establishment is out of control—of the people, of Congress, and of the presidents: Harry Truman, John Kennedy, Lyndon Johnson, Richard Nixon. So, on the campuses and elsewhere, and even in the White House, there are legitimate complaints about the establishment. And there is a great deal that must be changed.

To see the dimension of the complaints, look at the members of the establishment now under severe attack: Congress, by its own members; among others, the automobile industry, the aerospace industry, the press and television, the colleges, the food industry, the cosmetics and pharmaceuticals companies, the armament industry, the makers of napalm and other things, automobile insurers, pipeline companies, and on and on and on. It may have come to the point where you can't be a respectable member of the establishment unless you're under severe and sustained public attack.

And then there is, of course, the more generalized complaint directed at no specific part of the establishment: the complaint about the tinselly, plastic quality of American society. As somebody said of Hollywood years ago: to truly understand Hollywood, it is necessary to peel off the surface tinsel and find the real tinsel underneath. So what we see in our country today is an excited and confused uproar of charge and accusation plus, in some areas of the establishment, an excited and confused episode of self-examination.

The private areas of the American establishment do respond to criticism—slowly and painfully and after some resistance, but they do respond, and they are responding now. For example, the automobile industry now knows that if it doesn't stop making engines that pollute the air, it will soon be out of business. Other industries know that if they don't stop dumping mercury and other poisons in our waters, they're going to be closed down. That certainly is not to say that all the complaints against the private areas of the American establishment are being answered. It is to say that in the private areas of the establishment, as opposed to the government, there is some response. Ralph Nader has caused some changes in American life; yet he has never thrown a bomb or used violence in any form.

Now to return to our assumption that whoever blew up the lab at the University of Wisconsin acted out of what he thought were noble motives—an act of protest against an oppressive establishment and an unwieldy and unresponsive system. To some extent, whoever it was may have had the correct diagnosis. Our establishment is generally unresponsive. Not entirely, but to a great extent. He may have made the correct diagnosis, but he applied precisely the wrong cure. That kind of violence, or any kind of violence, will not do the job. On the contrary, it will guarantee that the job will not be done.

Violence will cause, and has already caused, a rigidly hostile public reaction, a conservative public reaction, a determination to protect the status quo even where there is wide agreement that the status quo needs to be changed. For example, one thing that needs to be changed, and soon, is the seniority—or geriatric, or senility—system in Congress. Even a lot of congressmen now believe this, some of whom stand to benefit by the seniority system. But the worst conceivable way to get Congress to change the seniority system is to try to force it by violence. Violence directed against the Congress would only guarantee that it would not be changed.

I suspect—I can't prove this, but neither can anyone disprove it —that most of the bombs now being exploded, on an average now of about three a day across the country, are not set off out of motives of nobility, to protest against an oppressive establishment. I suspect that there is a variety of other reasons much less noble than that—innate aggressiveness, a seeking of approval, sheer excitement and adventure, and perhaps in some cases for reasons of sexual inadequacy. In a society as pragmatic as ours, it is neither interesting nor informative to rail against violence on grounds of morality. The ultimate case against it simply is that it won't work —that in fact it will produce the opposite of the desired result. It will, literally and figuratively, blow up in your face.

It's easy enough for me to whine and complain about what is wrong, but—and this is a somewhat old-fashioned idea—I truly think that anyone who undertakes to criticize should offer some suggestions. I have two; one is somewhat fanciful, and the other is quite realistic. I will discuss the fanciful one first, not because I'm advocating it but because I think it is interesting.

Two years ago, when John Lindsay was running for reelection as mayor of New York City, some of you may recall that he used in his campaign the slogan "New York City spends more money on the war than it spends on New York City." And it does. If you take the federal taxes collected from the people of New York City, the portion of that spent in Vietnam is bigger than the budget of New York City. So, Lindsay was using this slogan to some effect. Some of his staff conceived the idea of having him say to the people of the city, "If I'm elected, the next time your federal income tax comes due, don't sent it to Washington; send it to City Hall, and there we will deduct what we think is a reasonable amount for education, health, welfare, police, fire, sanitation, and so on, and then we will send Washington what is left. And Washington can just make do with what it gets."

Had John Lindsay done this, their argument went—and had he got 20,000, 30,000, or 40,000 out of 7 million people in New York to do it—then Washington could not have done anything about it. You just can't put that many people in jail. They are violating the law, but they are not evading their taxes; they are paying their taxes, the full amount. They are simply insisting that the money be spent on what they think are their real needs before they start sending the money to Vietnam and paying subsidies to rich farmers and SSTs and that sort of thing.

Lindsay didn't go for it, and I bring it up only because I think it is interesting. If things continue as they are we might hear about it again. If New York City did it, it would only be a short time until it turned up in Chicago and Los Angeles and Baltimore and Philadelphia and Houston and Dallas.

The somewhat more realistic idea is this. In the spring of 1970, readers will recall, the Department of Commerce took the census for the first time by mail, almost entirely by mail. They sent these forms and they asked how many people are in the house and how much money do you make and how many bathtubs do you have, and so on. People checked off the answers in little boxes and mailed them in and the Census Bureau ran this through the computers and we are getting the answers, and it worked all right. It was fairly simple and accurate. What I suggest now is that this same kind of machinery now in existence be used every once in a while to ask the American people not how many bathtubs they have, but what they think and what they want and what they'd like and what they don't like.

Every few months, have the Census Bureau mail out a card with a few questions on it about whatever are the important issues at the time, asking people what they think. For two or three weeks before the day we could have a national discussion on television, on the radio, in the newspapers, in the magazines. Everybody involved in these questions and these issues should write what he thought and could say what he thought on the air. We could have debates and discussions explaining what the questions were about, saying what the alternatives were, what they would cost, what would happen if everyone voted yes, and what would happen if everyone voted no, to be sure that people knew what they were voting on. Then on a given day ask all the American people—not just 2,000 or 3,000 polled by George Gallup—to check off these cards and send them to the Census Bureau. Let them be run through the computers, and in a few days we'd have the answers.

Think about this. For the first time in human history a government would know exactly, precisely, honestly, and fairly what its people thought. No government has ever known what its people wanted since Athens was a small town, and the citizens walked down to the marketplace and voted by raising their hands on public questions (and even in Greece they had slaves and women who couldn't vote, so it wasn't truly democratic). The government has some sort of fuzzy idea. Congressmen go home on holidays and come back saying, well, I've talked to my people, and they think this and that. But what they mean is that maybe, if they've exerted themselves enormously, they might have talked to 1 percent of their constituents—in most cases, the country club set. So they don't know what the people want. We are never asked. I have been asked a number of times what one single person can do to influence events in this country, and the only answer I've ever been able to think of, and admittedly it is a very poor one, is to write to your congressman. Well, in some cases that works, some congressmen read their mail, and some respond to it and some don't. But even if they react to it, the mail to congressmen is so minuscule in terms of the total population that it is not a fair sample of American opinion.

Obviously the people's vote on these subjects, under the Constitution, would not be binding on Congress or the President. But it certainly ought to be influential. It would no longer be possible for a politician to say, "My people want this or that." We would know what his people wanted. We don't know now, we've never known before. While the vote would not be binding, it would be so substantial and so authoritative that it would become a kind of bench mark for politicians. Those who wanted to serve the American people would then know how to do it, and those who did not could go home. So, two suggestions, one fanciful, one realistic. And I think they might even work.

I am not sure that we always understand the severe damage that has been done to our society by the crime and the violence that have happened in this country. I have heard a little anecdote which illustrates it brilliantly, I think. A young man who worked for me in Washington was driving home some months ago, and on the curb he saw two young men, about twenty years old, hitchhiking. They were holding up a home-made paper sign saying, "We are British." He thought that was interesting, so he stopped to pick them up. They were British college students who had spent the summer in this country hitchhiking coast-to-coast and keeping careful records on what they had seen and heard with the intention of writing theses about it when they went back to school in the fall. They were such nice people that he brought them into the office the next day, and we gave them a little work to do to give them a little money to help them along. I talked to them for a while, and one of them said they had been given something like 798 rides. During these rides from town to town across the country they had, of course, talked to the Americans who had picked them up, and in these 798 conversations, sooner or later, 98 percent of the drivers had said, "You know, if you were American I wouldn't have picked you up." Doesn't that tell it?

The system is slow. God knows it's slow. It's cumbersome. It's often unfair. But the alternative is unspeakable. And despite our British hitchhikers' poll, there is an essential decency and an essential fairness in the American people that lies beneath their fears. If it is appealed to, honestly and persuasively, there is the power to change our society for the better. Bombs will change it, but only for the worse. When we think of the changes we want, we should also think of the changes we don't want. There are many great things in this country: bookstores, bicycles, dogwood trees, bumper stickers, wild daisies, LP records, beer and pizza, canoes, Colorado, and people we like. It's worth saving.

9

ON CIVIL OBEDIENCE

AND DISOBEDIENCE

Introduction: On December 2, 1970, the philosopher Charles Frankel and the historian Howard Zinn engaged in a debate at The Johns Hopkins University. Reading from a prepared text, Professor Frankel led off with a systematic and largely critical analysis of the dimensions and implications of civil disobedience. Occasionally his remarks were directed personally at Professor Zinn, and particularly at his most recent book, *Disobedience and Democracy: Nine Fallacies on Law and Order.* In his extemporaneous reply, Mr. Zinn chose to ignore Mr. Frankel's attacks upon his book and, like a train passing in the night, he directed his attention instead to what he viewed as the conservative and frequently brutalizing implications of the sanctified canons of civil obedience that inequitable social orders—and particularly ours—have historically cultivated to defend the status quo. In their rejoinders both scholars clashed more directly and more heatedly. The question of who got the best of it is reserved for the reader, in whose interest both slightly revised their remarks for publication in this volume.

charles frankel

SOME CIVIL THOUGHTS ABOUT
CIVIL DISOBEDIENCE

No ONE WHO BELIEVES, with the Declaration of Independence, that there are circumstances in which men have a moral right to struggle, even illegally, against abuses perpetrated by a government can take an absolutistic position against civil disobedience. It cannot, of course, be a legal right; that would be a contradiction in terms. But there are times, places, and causes that make civil disobedience morally justifiable. This can, I think, be accepted as the point of departure for discussion.

Charles Frankel is Old Dominion Professor of Philosophy and Public Affairs at Columbia University, and he is also editor-at-large for *Saturday Review*. He served as assistant secretary of state for educational and cultural affairs from 1965 through 1967. His publications include *High on Foggy Bottom* (New York: Harper & Row, 1969); *The Democratic Prospect* (New York: Harper & Row, 1962); *The Case for Modern Man* (New York: Harper, 1956); and *The Faith of Reason* (New York: King's Crown Press, 1948).

But the beginning of the problem of civil disobedience, looked at philosophically, is that many people mistake the beginning of the problem for the end of it. As the Declaration of Independence also says, the rejection of the authority of a long-established government is a serious matter. A decent respect for the opinions of mankind requires that very good reasons be given for embarking on such a course of behavior. My purpose here is to try to suggest, though it must be in a brief form, the kind of thinking in which, I believe, we must engage—the sorts of questions we must ask and answers we must seek—if we are to come to reasonable and conscientious judgments on the issues that civil disobedience poses.

I know of no political subject so difficult to discuss today. On its own intellectual merits the subject is difficult. Examination of it requires subtle distinctions, sympathy with feelings and ideas that are likely to be strongly opposed to one's own, and sensitivity to a broad range of social values, many of which are likely to be forgotten amidst the pressures and passions of the moment. The combination of analytic care, empathy, and sageness which the discussion of civil disobedience demands is very rare, which is one reason why the subject is in a disordered intellectual condition.

But it is not the only reason. Civil disobedience, by its very nature, invites not argument but epithets, not moral discrimination but moral posturing. It does so whether you favor a particular act of civil disobedience or oppose it. This is because civil disobedience is commonly thought to be justified only if one has very strong convictions on a subject. But strong convictions, though they frequently need analysis even more than weak ones, resist such analysis. Moreover, they provoke strong convictions in return. And so one ends up in a bind. Merely to ask questions about civil disobedience, either pro or contra, is to suggest that one does not have the strong convictions one ought to have. One seems equivocal where he should be firm, insensitive or immoral where sensitivity and morality are the heart of the matter.

To make the matter worse, civil disobedience has become encumbered with a vocabulary that hides issues instead of revealing them. One of the words that makes trouble, for example, is "conscience." I do not believe, of course, that a man should act against his conscience. No one does. At least I don't believe it, and no one believes it, until we give thought to the curious kinds of conscience that some people seem to have. Do we think that George Wallace should act in accordance with his conscience? Or do we think that it would be better to persuade him to act in accordance with the Supreme Court's interpretation of the law of the land? To invoke the individual conscience as a final court of appeal is basic to most defenses of civil disobedience. But it is an incomplete defense unless we also say whose conscience is to be the court, and why, and what we mean by "conscience" in the first place. And all this takes us beyond conscience to something else—to what I would like to call "conscientiousness." It demands the careful definition of terms, the examination of facts, the weighing of consequences, and the willingness to deal as seriously, at least at the beginning, with other people's beliefs, concerns, and moral convictions as one does with one's own.

Indeed, I find myself puzzled by many of those who currently speak of "conscience" as the single or supreme sanction for their acts. Large numbers of these people are secular humanists who do not seek a divine sanction for morals. But individual conscience as a moral sanction was introduced by people who believed that God spoke directly to the individual soul. To disobey conscience was to disobey His word. If we separate conscience from these theological beliefs, why should we give it superior authority? In the end, it is true, a man has no alternative but to use his own judgment in appraising social and moral issues, and must take responsibility for his acts insofar as he has an effective choice about them. He has to do this even if his best judgment is that he should follow the judgment of someone else. But this is not to say that each man's personal judgment has some sort of natural intellectual or moral superiority over the judgments of the courts, the electorate, or the general opinion of mankind. It may be right when all these are wrong. But it need not be, and unless we think that God speaks to us, but not to those who disagree with us, there is no reason to make a fetish of our private judgments.

This tendency to overplay the claims of individual conscience, without examining the whys and wherefores, seems to me to be present, if I may say so, in much that Mr. Zinn has had to say on the subject of civil disobedience, although my judgment, of course, is not infallible. He draws an antithesis between the individual and government in *Disobedience and Democracy* which I can only think he would wish to retract: "In our reasoning about civil disobedience," he writes, "we must never forget that we and the state are separate in our interests, and we must not be lured into forgetting this by the agents of the state. The state seeks power, influence, wealth, as ends in themselves. The individual seeks health, peace, creative activity, love." I ask each man and women to look at his neighbor, to look at himself, and to ask if he recognises this paragon of individual good will whom Mr. Zinn draws.

"The individual seeks health, peace, creative activity, love." Never any fast cars that are injurious to health? No love of excitement, and even some enjoyment of violence? All creative activity and no desire just to put one's feet up? No irritation at other people's creative activities, like the supersonic transport? All love, and no aggression, fears, vanities, or hatred of people who won't love others as one thinks they should? I am not being cynical; I think I enjoy my fellow men, and that I have some affection for them. But I think it is possible to be sentimental about abstractions called "the individual," and that this sentimentality has the same pragmatic consequence as cynicism: it prevents us from taking men seriously for what they are and from being attached to them for what they are.

It also prevents us, if I may now get on more dangerous ground, from taking a demystified view of government and the state. A mystique of the state lies behind much that is said by supporters of civil disobedience, just as it lies behind the excesses of patrioteering and totalitarianism. Immediately following the words I have just quoted, Mr. Zinn says, for example: "The state, because of its power and wealth, has no end of spokesmen for its interests. This means the citizen must understand the need to think and act on his own in concert with fellow citizens." Well, there are some states—I think of those in the poorer parts of the world —that almost certainly think that they have an inadequate supply of spokesmen for their interests, whether on the home scene or in the international arena. And I am not persuaded that Lyndon Johnson had an endless number of spokesmen for his interests, or that Mr. Nixon, during the Cambodian crisis, was overwhelmed by the support he received. States are in a contest for power, influence, wealth, and some governments and states can marshal awesome amounts of these things. But many also find that they can lose these things rapidly. I think we would do better to talk not about a Platonic abstraction, the state or the government, but about particular states, which are mortal human creations with historical careers and not rigid forces immune to the perils of existence.

Indeed, we might reflect on what Mr. Zinn says in the sentence that follows his apotheosizing of the state. He speaks of the citizen thinking and acting on his own or in concert with fellow citizens. Suppose—merely suppose for the purpose of argument— that a group of us thought and acted together, and came, *mirabile dictu*, to some agreement, and managed to concert successfully with other citizens, and came eventually, greatest miracle of all, to be the dominant party in the government. Would we then be prepared to say what Mr. Zinn says about the inherent difference between the state and the individual? Or would we then be proclaiming that the state, of course, seeks only health, peace, creative activity and love, and that it is the individual—specifically those so obtuse as not to believe in our good motives—who seeks power, influence, and wealth as ends in themselves? Of course, you may not think that you can ever, by acting in concert with other citizens, affect a government or become a dominant force in it. And perhaps you are right: you may lack the wit and the will, or the numbers or the money. But this is a judgment based on the examination of specific facts and not on a metaphysical disjunction between conscience and the devil, the individual and the state. It puts the question of your relation to the state on an entirely different terrain.

Now what do all these questions add up to? They add up, I suggest, to the view that what we are discussing when we discuss civil disobedience is politics. I do not mean that we are not discussing morals. Politics affects some of the most important values of life. But civil disobedience is politics in the sense that it is actions that are part of a contest in which some people have views or interests or ideals that they want to make prevail and other people, out of inertia, inattention, or positive opposition, are preventing this from happening. When we face a contest like this, we have to ask political questions. Even if there is sometimes a moral right to civil disobedience, this does not make each act of civil disobedience right. We have to look at any particular claim to the moral right of civil disobedience with a cold, analytical eye, and it should be a political eye.

If we do look at acts of civil disobedience in this way, what are the issues they pose? The first is to recognize that there are different kinds of civil disobedience, which pose different issues. At one time it was easier to say what was meant by "civil disobedience" than it is now. The phenomenon has faded into others that used to be separated from it, and the label "civil disobedience" has come to designate categories of action significantly different in the scope, intensity, and purpose of the disobedience involved.

Broadly, I suggest that there are four categories of "civil disobedience," using the word so as to allow anything that claims to be civil disobedience to be so labeled. The simplest and most usual kind is what I would call "issue-oriented" civil disobedience. It has to do with some specific and limited matter which, it is thought, justifies disobedience to the law. In this category there are three subclasses. Sometimes men break a law in order to test its validity. They disobey it in order to institute proceedings in the courts which will decide whether the law is constitutional and whether they were in fact lawbreakers. In effect, this is not a challenge to the legal system but an effort to use it to effect remedies of what is felt to be objectionable. A second kind of issue-oriented civil disobedience represents an effort not to change a law but simply to detach oneself from its effects. A man may find a law requiring racial segregation an intolerable indignity; another may regard a law requiring him to fight in a particular war as a commandment to be personally immoral. Such men may disobey not to launch a struggle against the evils they find obnoxious but only because they personally refuse to cooperate with these evils. Finally, there is a kind of civil disobedience which is intended to begin a chain of events which will remove an area of grievous evil.

Now all these types of issue-oriented civil disobedience—and of course they frequently overlap—have two characteristics in common. First, they are not intended to overthrow an existing government or legal system but only to change one disturbing part of it. Second, they are committed to nonviolence. This is usually a voluntary commitment on the part of those who practice civil disobedience of this sort, but I think it is also a probabilistic inference from the partial and limited character of the objectives involved. If you practice violence, you spread out into other issues, and you challenge the legal system at one of its most crucial points. Success not only invites other violence but delivers the authority of the legal system a heavy blow. So we may take it that civil disobedience in this first category raises questions only within the framework of the existing system of law and government, and its justification must be sought within that framework.

How do we go about seeking its justification? By asking, I suggest, the following kind of question: Will it work? What will be its other consequences even if it does work? What are the alternatives to it? Most important of all, does it endanger the existing system, or does it, as is sometimes possible, strengthen it by removing some of the causes for serious grievances against it? In my view, the evidence, in general, comes down against civil disobedience, even of this restricted sort. The stakes we have in a functioning legal system—and I mean by "we" practically all of us who live in this country—are very great. Among its benefits are a measure of predictability in our fellows' behavior; protection against private violence and aggression; a framework for peaceful cooperation and adjustment of disputes; a set of identifiable procedures for determining, in a confused world, what the public interest, for the moment, will be defined as being; and, in constitutionally governed societies, at least a few moderately effective procedures for protecting ourselves from arbitrary acts by people in authority. These may seem small benefits. Those who have them are likely to take them for granted. But most people in history have lived without them, and large numbers of people would consider them today to be very great and revolutionary benefits indeed. Nevertheless, there are cases where the impact of a social ill on a particular individual or group, or on the viability and justice of the legal system taken as a whole, may be so acute that the risks involved in calculated but limited disobedience may be worth taking. I think there have been justified instances of civil disobedience in recent history even in the face of the consideration that the burden of moral proof rests on the supporters of civil disobedience.

The larger issues now posed by civil disobedience, however, come from confusing the kind of disobedience that I have been talking about with other kinds. Issue-oriented civil disobedience very easily fades into what I would call "coercive disobedience." Here we have a kind of conduct which is still focused on particular issues but which uses disobedience in such a way as to affect other people's rights and to deny them the freedom to follow their own conscience. Prevention of the use of university buildings or public facilities is an example. By what right do the coercively disobedient directly impose the authority of their consciences on others? Perhaps there are grounds, but plainly, they have to be even stronger than in the case of the first kind of civil disobedience. Moreover, what is the principle of action on which such tactics are based? That anyone with a conscientiously held view on some matter may nonviolently stop others with different conscientious views from doing what they think right?

And this leads to still another question: What is the purpose, the goal, the end-in-view of this coercion? Do we mean, in universities, for example, that universities should make collective political judgments quite independently of the regular political processes, with which all their members are forced to cooperate? And do we mean they shall make these under the threat that they will be closed if they don't? How, then, will we argue for the right to conduct our individual business in universities as we please against those who might wish to coerce us into adopting a collective political stance on the other side from ours? Coercive civil disobedience, as in the case of factory sit-ins in the thirties, had a specific objective—the establishment of the principle of collective bargaining. Is the organization of a university into political blocs a desirable objective in the same way? If you think so, at least we know where you stand; you think that universities should have a party line. If you think not, coercive civil disobedience on a university campus is intolerable.

Perhaps this is why the case for coercive civil disobedience almost inevitably fades into a case for something else. This is a third category of civil disobedience, the best name for which is probably "passive resistance." This is conduct nonviolent in character but aimed not at the removal of specific evils within a legal framework that one accepts but rather at the removal of that framework and the substitution of a new one for it. Gandhi's tactics of opposition to the British raj are the model example. I do not wish to quibble over whether "passive resistance" of the broad kind intended to bring down a regime and replace it with another should or shouldn't be called a version of "civil disobedience." This is a purely semantic issue. The important question is the logic that one should follow if one wants to decide whether, in a particular case, actions with such a purpose are justified. This logic is not the same as with acts of civil disobedience oriented to specific issues.

In the first place, one has to have a theory of political legitimacy. If one wishes to overthrow an existing regime, one has to ask, for example, whether it rests, so far as one can tell, on the consent of a majority of the governed. If it does, on what grounds should it be overthrown? On the grounds that the majority are misled? In that case, you must hold an elitist theory of political legitimacy; you must think it perfectly all right to impose your will on the majority when it has proved itself so stupid as not to be persuaded by your views. Or do you perhaps think that the majority really wants what you want but doesn't know it, because it has been manipulated by a minority? If so, you have to produce arguments showing, first, that this really is the case and, second, that if you win, the minority you represent will not do the same. Moreover, you have to show you won't engage in the same process of overt or disguised repression. And you have to explain how the evils you seek to cure by substituting one form of minority regime for another will be cured by this device, and that this cure won't be worse than the original disease.

A second and equally grave issue is thus involved. Whatever your theory of political legitimacy, you also have to have some notion in mind of the regime you wish to erect in place of the regime you are trying to bring down. I am aware of the argument that one cannot ask for a bill of particulars, describing just what one will do in circumstances that one cannot predict. But I do not ask for a bill of particulars; I merely ask for a rough sketch, and an answer to a few minimal questions. How will the regime be set up? How will its leaders be chosen? What powers of recall will there be? Who will have them? And how do you propose to get for it the support it needs to collect taxes, make laws that will be obeyed, and do the other things that regimes must do? Marx, in a very general way, did have answers to these questions; whether they were good or not is beside the present point. And so did Gandhi. If you do not have answers to such questions, you are undertaking a course of behavior that can have dire consequences for your friends as well as your adversaries, and you are doing this, you must yourself admit, without serious thought about these consequences. I find difficulty attaching the word "conscientious" to such behavior.

I recognize that many who ally themselves with notions of passive resistance think such questions beside the point. Once the present repressive regime has disappeared, it will be replaced by no regime at all. Perhaps only voluntary associations, each doing their own thing, will exist. There will be no problems of monetary stability or environmental pollution or public health. Laws will be replaced by personal and informal controls (excluding lynching, I suppose), everyone will have the freedom of the freest free entrepreneur but nobody will be exploited and everyone's budget will be balanced. And the police, if they are needed, will grow naturally and spontaneously, like roses, from the communal vines. They will spring from the people, which is something they don't do now. Perhaps it is best that those who have such hopes are shy about spelling out their political ideas. It shows that they have some discretion despite their valor.

This is why I am unimpressed by people who announce that they have "consciences" and then talk loosely about "tearing down the system." If they wish to replace something they choose to call capitalism with something they will call socialism, that is a possible ideal, but it is a separate matter. If they are indignant and nauseated by the interminable cruelty of Vietnam and can see no reason that justifies the violence our government is employing in that country, that, too, is another issue. Strong remedies are plainly needed, and they may involve, before we are through, far-reaching reforms in the structure of our political parties and in the distribution of money and power in the government and the country at large. The only question at stake is whether these changes should be brought about by nonconstitutional means. If that is the issue, then one must, I think, deal with the kind of questions I have raised. They are tough questions, but I think they are fair. My own judgment, for what it is worth, is that a conscientious democrat (with a small "d") who asks himself these questions will come out thinking that a nonconstitutional change of regime is neither a legitimate nor a realistic plan of action.

I realize that what I have said may invite the rejoinder that, for the sake of peaceful and orderly governmental procedures in this country, I am willing to allow our country to visit untold suffering on people in Vietnam or elsewhere. But this is not a rejoinder; it begs the operative questions: Can another regime be installed? How? What will it be capable of doing? I do not think that the answer to these questions will encourage the hope that passive resistance is a technique for a lessening of the suffering in the world. Indeed, the most likely outcome of a really threatening campaign of widespread passive resistance (which is a hypothesis that is, in itself, not easy to entertain) would probably be the installation of a government of hawks, not of doves. Nor is it an answer to say, as has often been said, that other methods have been tried and haven't worked. Sometimes they haven't been seriously tried; sometimes they have worked; and, in any case, their failure doesn't prove that any other method is better. The most obvious consequence of talk and effort concentrated on such tactics is the draining of energy and intelligence into dreams and attitudinizing and away from actions that may have an effect in shortening the war.

Which brings me to the final category of civil disobedience, so-called. This is the technique of breaking the law which, though it may for tactical reasons avoid violence at the moment, nevertheless has no principled objection to violence. It conceives civil disobedience as a step to passive resistance; and it conceives passive resistance as the preparation for revolutionary violence. Everything that I have said about passive resistance, it seems to me, applies, doubled, to this approach. It does not simply underestimate the dangers of violence that can be provoked by nonviolence, which is one of the errors of those who speak for passive resistance. It actively courts these dangers, and it does so either with no theory of political legitimacy or with one that is nine-tenths bombast; it courts these dangers, furthermore, with a program for government that cannot be reasonably thought to be a viable or even a seriously intended program. Rosa Luxembourg, who had some credentials as a serious revolutionary, thought it the height of irresponsibility to call a general strike for small cause or for any cause in which the strike had no plausible chance of achieving its purpose. She thought it wicked to destroy decent hopes by quixotic actions. It *is* wicked; indeed, it is more wicked when the hopes that are destroyed are decent ones.

So I think the issue narrows down to the kind of civil disobedience I called "issue-oriented." And I think that what has happened over the last few years is that the limited and difficult case that can sometimes be made for civil disobedience of this sort has been obscured and weakened by the loosening of the principles that should govern it. It has faded into other more dangerous, and much more morally dubious, kinds of conduct. Its own commitment to nonviolence has been embarrassed by the violence it has over time encouraged. The case for it, therefore, is now weaker than it was. Today, there are probabilities of violence which can be touched off by nonviolent disobedience that are much higher than a decade or even a half-decade ago. We have to try in some way to work our way back. If we are to recover a case for civil disobedience, we have to recover clarity in defining it, and we have to be firm against those who exploit and corrupt it in careless ignorance or in fanatical indifference.

howard zinn

THE PROBLEM IS CIVIL OBEDIENCE

I START FROM THE SUPPOSITION that the world is topsy-turvy, that things are all wrong, that the wrong people are in jail and the wrong people are out of jail, that the wrong people are in power and the wrong people are out of power, that the wealth is distributed in this country and the world in such a way as not simply to require small reform but to require a drastic reallocation of wealth. I start from the supposition that we don't have to say too

Howard Zinn is professor of government at Boston University. A native of New York City, he graduated from New York University and received his Ph.D. in history from Columbia University in 1958. From 1956 to 1963 he was chairman of the History Department at Spelman College, and in 1958 he received the Albert J. Beveridge Prize from the American Historical Association for *La Guardia in Congress* (Ithaca, N.Y.; Cornell University Press, 1959). His other publications include *SNCC: The New Abolitionists* (Boston: Beacon Press, 1964); *The Southern Mystique* (New York: Knopf, 1964); *Vietnam: The Logic of Withdrawal* (Boston: Beacon Press, 1967); *Disobedience and Democracy: Nine Fallacies on Law and Order* (New York: Random House, 1968); and *The Politics of History* (Boston: Beacon Press, 1970).

154

much about this because all we have to do is think about the state of the world today and realize that things are all upside down.

Daniel Berrigan is in jail—a Catholic priest, a poet who opposes the war—and J. Edgar Hoover is free, you see. David Dellinger, who has opposed war ever since he was this high and who has used all of his energy and passion against it, is in danger of going to jail. The men who are responsible for the My Lai massacre are not on trial; they are in Washington serving various functions, primary and subordinate, that have to do with the unleashing of massacres, which surprise them when they occur. At Kent State University four students were killed by the National Guard and the students were indicted. In every city in this country, when demonstrations take place, the protestors, whether they have demonstrated or not, whatever they have done, are assaulted and clubbed by police, and then they are arrested for assaulting a police officer.

Now I have been studying very closely what happens every day in the courts in Boston, Massachusetts. You would be astounded —maybe you wouldn't, maybe you have been around, maybe you have lived, maybe you have thought, maybe you have been hit —at how the daily rounds of injustice make their way through this marvelous thing that we call due process. Well, that is my premise.

All you have to do is read the Soledad letters of George Jackson, who was sentenced to one year to life of which he spent ten years, for a 70-dollar robbery of a filling station. And then there is the U.S. Senator who is alleged to keep 185,000 dollars a year, or something like that, on the oil depletion allowance. One is theft; the other is legislation. Something is wrong, something is terribly wrong when we ship 10,000 bombs full of nerve gas across the country, and drop them in somebody else's swimming pool so as not to trouble our own. So you lose your perspective after a while. If you don't think, if you just listen to TV and read scholarly things, you actually begin to think that things are not so bad, or that just little things are wrong. But you have to get a little detached, and then come back and look at the world, and you are horrified. So we have to start from that supposition—that things are really topsy-turvy.

And our topic is topsy-turvy: civil disobedience. As soon as you say the topic is civil disobedience, you are saying our *problem* is civil disobedience. That is *not* our problem. Our problem is civil *obedience*. Our problem is the numbers of people all over the world who have obeyed the dictates of the leaders of their government and have gone to war, and millions have been killed because of this obedience. And our problem is that scene in *All Quiet on the Western Front* where the schoolboys march off dutifully in a line to war. Our problem is that people are obedient all over the world, in the face of poverty and starvation and stupidity, and war, and cruelty. Our problem is that people are obedient while the jails are full of petty thieves, and all the while the grand thieves are running the country. That's our problem. We recognize this for Nazi Germany. We know that the problem there was obedience, that the people obeyed Hitler. People obeyed; that was wrong. They should have challenged and they should have resisted, and if we were only there, we would have showed them. Even in Stalin's Russia we can understand that; people are obedient, all these herdlike people.

But America is different. That is what we've all been brought up on. From the time we are this high—and I still hear it resounding in Mr. Frankel's statement—you tick off, one, two, three, four, five lovely things about America that we don't want disturbed very much.

But if we have learned anything in the past ten years it is that these lovely things about America were never lovely. We have been expansionist and aggressive and mean to other people from the beginning. And we've been aggressive and mean to people in *this* country, and we've allocated the wealth of this country in a very unjust way. We've never had justice in the courts for the poor people, for black people, for radicals. Now how can we boast that America is a very special place? It is not that special. It really isn't.

Well, that is our topic, that is our problem: civil obedience. Law is very important. We are talking about obedience to law—

law, this marvelous invention of modern times, which we attribute to Western civilization, and which we talk about proudly. The rule of law, oh, how wonderful, all these courses in Western civilization all over the land. Remember those bad old days when people were exploited by feudalism? Everything was terrible in the Middle Ages—but now we have Western civilization, the rule of law. *The rule of law has regularized and maximized the injustice that existed before the rule of law, that is what the rule of law has done.* Let us start looking at the rule of law realistically, not with that metaphysical complacency with which we always examined it before.

When in all the nations of the world the rule of law is the darling of the leaders and the plague of the people we ought to begin to recognize this. We have to transcend these national boundaries in our thinking. Nixon and Brezhnev have much more in common with one another than we have with Nixon. J. Edgar Hoover has far more in common with the head of the Soviet secret police than he has with us. It's the international dedication to law and order that binds the leaders of all countries in a comradely bond. That's why we are always surprised when they get together—they smile, they shake hands, they smoke cigars, they really like one another no matter what they say. It's like the Republican and Democratic parties, who claim that it's going to make a terrible difference if one or the other wins, yet they are all the same. Basically it is us against them.

Yossarian was right, remember, in *Catch-22*? He had been accused of giving aid and comfort to the enemy, which nobody should ever be accused of, and Yossarian said to his friend Clevinger: "The enemy is whoever is going to get you killed, whichever side they are on." But that didn't sink in, so he said to Clevinger: "Now you remember that, or one of these days you'll be dead." And remember? Clevinger, after a while, was dead. And we must remember that our enemies are not divided along national lines, that enemies are not just people who speak different languages and occupy different territories. Enemies are people who want to get us killed.

We are asked, "What if everyone disobeyed the law?" But a better question is, "What if everyone obeyed the law?" And the answer to that question is much easier to come by, because we have a lot of empirical evidence about what happens if everyone obeys the law, or if even most people obey the law. What happens is what has happened, what is happening. Why do people revere the law? And we all do; even I have to fight it, for it was put into my bones at an early age when I was a Cub Scout. One reason we revere the law is its ambivalence. In the modern world we deal with phrases and words that have multiple meanings, like "national security." Oh, yes, we must do this for national security! Well, what does that mean? Whose national security? Where? When? Why? We don't bother to answer those questions, or even to ask them.

The law conceals many things. The law is the Bill of Rights. In fact that is what we think of when we develop our reverence for the law. The law is something that protects us; the law is our right— the law is the Constitution. Bill of Rights Day, essay contests sponsored by the American Legion on our Bill of Rights, that is the law. And that is good.

But there is another part of the law that doesn't get ballyhooed —the legislation that has gone through month after month, year after year, from the beginning of the Republic, which allocates the resources of the country in such a way as to leave some people very rich and other people very poor, and the other people scrambling like mad for what little is left. That is the law. If you go to a law school you will see this. You can quantify it by counting the big, heavy law books that people carry around with them and see how many law books you count that say "Constitutional Rights" on them and how many that say "Property," "Contracts," "Torts," "Corporation Law." That is what the law is mostly about. The law is the oil depletion allowance—although we don't have Oil Depletion Allowance Day, we don't have essays written on behalf of the oil depletion allowance. So there are parts of the law that are publicized and played up to us—oh, this is the law, the Bill of Rights. And there are other parts of the law that just do their quiet work, and nobody says anything about them.

It started way back. When the Bill of Rights was first passed, remember in the first administration of Washington? Great thing, Bill of Rights passed! Big ballyhoo. At the same time Hamilton's economic program was passed. Nice, quiet, money to the rich— I'm simplifying it a little, but not too much. Hamilton's economic program started it off. You can draw a straight line from Hamilton's economic program to the oil depletion allowance and to the tax write-offs for corporations. All the way through—that is the history. The Bill of Rights publicized; economic legislation unpublicized.

You know the enforcement of different parts of the law is as important as the publicity attached to the different parts of the law. The Bill of Rights, is it enforced? Not very well. You'll find that freedom of speech in constitutional law is a very difficult, ambiguous, troubled concept. Nobody really knows when you can get up and speak and when you can't. Just check all of the Supreme Court decisions. Talk about predictability in a system—you can't predict what will happen to you when you get up on the street corner and speak. See if you can tell the difference between the Terminiello case and the Feiner case, and see if you can figure out what is going to happen. By the way, there is one part of the law that is not very vague, and that involves the right to distribute leaflets on the street. The Supreme Court has been very clear on that. In decision after decision we are affirmed an absolute right to distribute leaflets on the street. Try it. Just go out on the street and start distributing leaflets. And a policeman comes up to you and he says, "Get out of here." And you say, "Aha!—Do you know *Marsh* v. *Alabama*, 1946?" That is the reality of the Bill of Rights. That's the reality of the Constitution, that part of the law which is portrayed to us as a beautiful and marvelous thing. And seven years after the Bill of Rights was passed, which said that "Congress shall make no law abridging the freedom of speech," Congress made a law abridging the freedom of speech. Remember? The Sedition Act of 1798.

So the Bill of Rights was not enforced. Hamilton's program was enforced, because when the whisky farmers went out and rebelled, you remember, in 1794 in Pennsylvania, Hamilton himself got on his horse and went out there to suppress the rebellion to make sure that the revenue tax was enforced. And you can trace the story right down to the present day, what laws are enforced, what laws are not enforced. So you have to be careful when you say, "I'm for the law, I revere the law." What part of the law are you talking about? I'm not against all law. But I think we ought to begin to make very important distinctions about what laws do what things to what people.

And there are other problems with the law. It's a strange thing, we think that law brings order. Law doesn't. How do we know that law does not bring order? Look around us. We live under the rules of law. Notice how much order we have? People say we have to worry about civil disobedience because it will lead to anarchy. Take a look at the present world in which the rule of law obtains. This is the closest to what is called anarchy in the popular mind—confusion, chaos, international banditry. The only order that is really worth anything does not come through the enforcement of law, it comes through the establishment of a society which is just and in which harmonious relationships are established and in which you need a minimum of regulation to create decent sets of arrangements among people. But the order based on law and on the *force* of law is the order of the totalitarian state, and it inevitably leads either to total injustice or to rebellion—eventually, in other words, to very great disorder.

We all grow up with the notion that the law is holy. They asked Daniel Berrigan's mother what she thought of her son's breaking the law. He burned draft records—one of the most violent acts of this century—to protest the war, for which he was sentenced to prison, as criminals should be. They asked his mother, who is in her eighties, what she thought of her son's breaking the law. And she looked straight into the interviewer's face, and she said, "It's not God's law." Now we forget that. There is nothing sacred about the law. Think of who makes laws. The law is not made by

God, it is made by Strom Thurmond. If you have any notion about the sanctity and loveliness and reverence for the law, look at the legislators around the country who make the laws. Sit in on the sessions of the state legislatures. Sit in on Congress, for these are the people who make the laws which we are then supposed to revere.

All of this is done with such propriety as to fool us. This is the problem. In the old days things were confused, you didn't know. Now you know. It is all down there in the books. Now we go through due process. Now the same things happen as happened before, except that we've gone through the right procedures. In Boston a policeman walked into a hospital ward and fired five times at a black man who had snapped a towel at his arm—and killed him. A hearing was held. The judge decided that the policeman was justified because if he didn't do it he would lose the respect of his fellow officers. Well, that is what is known as due process—that is, the guy didn't get away with it. We went through the proper procedures and everything was set up. The decorum, the propriety of the law fools us.

The nation, then, was founded on disrespect for the law, and then came the Constitution and the notion of stability which Madison and Hamilton liked. But then we found in certain crucial times in our history that the legal framework did not suffice, and in order to end slavery we had to go outside the legal framework, as we had to do at the time of the American Revolution. The unions had to go outside the legal framework in order to establish certain rights in the 1930s. And in this time, which may be more critical than the time of the Revolution or the Civil War, the problems are so horrendous as to require us to go outside the legal framework in order to make a statement, to resist, to begin to establish the kind of institutions and relationships which a decent society should have. No, not just tearing things down; building things up. But even if you build things up that you are not supposed to build up —you try to build up a people's park, that's not tearing down a system; you are building something up, but you are doing it illegally—the militia comes in and drives you out. That is the form that civil disobedience is going to take more and more, people trying to build a new society in the midst of the old.

But what about voting and elections? Civil disobedience—we don't need that much of it, we are told, because we can go through the electoral system. And by now we should have learned, but maybe we haven't, for we grew up with the notion that the voting booth is a sacred place, almost like a confessional. You walk into the voting booth and you come out and they snap your picture and they put it in the papers with a beatific smile on your face. You've just voted; that is democracy. But if you even read what the political scientists say—although who can?—about the voting process, you find that the voting process is a sham. Totalitarian states love voting. You get people to the polls and they register their approval. I know there is a difference, they have one party and we have two parties. We have one more party than they have, you see.

What we are trying to do, I assume, is really to get back to the principles and aims and spirit of the Declaration of Independence. This spirit is resistance to illegitimate authority and to forces that deprive people of their life and liberty and right to pursue happiness, and therefore under these conditions it urges the right to alter or abolish their current form of government—and the stress has been on abolish. But to establish the principles of the Declaration of Independence we are going to need to go outside the law, to stop obeying the laws that demand killing or that allocate wealth the way it has been done or that put people in jail for petty technical offenses and keep other people out of jail for enormous crimes. My hope is that this kind of spirit will take place not just in this country but in other countries because they all need it. People in all countries need the spirit of disobedience to the state, which is not a metaphysical thing but a thing of force and wealth. And we need a kind of declaration of interdependence among peoples in all countries of the world who are striving for the same thing.

REJOINDERS

Mr. Frankel replies: My wife said to me the other day, "How does it happen that no matter where you go you always seem to end up in the minority?" I was in the minority when I was in the government, and then when I came out I returned to Columbia University and I turned out to be in what seemed the minority there, and I seem to be in the minority here. That is all right. That is the penalty one pays for being right. It is a well-known fact about majorities that at any given time they see one thing very clearly and nothing else and that they leave their children to pick up the pieces.

I predicted, when I started, that civil disobedience was a difficult subject to discuss because it involves strong feelings. And if you raise any questions about it, the suggestion is made that you don't have the strong feelings you ought to have. In my paper I said little about the evils of the world, but I think I know about them. I think many of us do. I am not and have never been supine or complacent about these evils. But among the evils that have brought us to our present condition is fanaticism. What is the sign of fanaticism? The best sign is the belief that if a man disagrees with you about the best means to achieve an end he can't really want that end. To take an example, I think, as Mr. Zinn does, that it is unjust that some people should be rich and the great majority of the world very poor. It is brutally unjust. The question, however, is what to do about it. I am not convinced that reducing the power of government to act in relation to the economy is the way to do it. That belief isn't a matter of conscience. It is a matter on which I would hope honorable men could disagree.

I find myself confused by people who, on the one side, deplore poverty and injustice in the strongest terms and demand that immediate action be taken to remove them and then, on the other side, say that government is, on principle, to be distrusted and disobeyed. I think that only a strong government, one whose authority is habitually accepted by the citizenry, can marshal the power to do something effective about poverty and injustice. I do not say that it *will* do so; I say only that if it doesn't, we aren't likely to find any other agency capable of dealing with the problem. So I think it puzzling to condemn government as such and to spread the idea that "individuals" are inherently good while "government" is inherently bad. There are bad individuals in government; there are cliques, cabals, groups, within it that may destroy its power to do good and make it do evil; but there is no way to deal with these obstacles except to work in and through government, and on it, to change it. The idea of general resistance to it seems to me an excuse, unwitting perhaps, but nevertheless an excuse, for a cop-out.

But this disagreement with Mr. Zinn, and with the many who seem to agree with him, is a disagreement about means, not about ends. I do not suppose that those who disagree with me on the matter are immoral because they do; I have no reason to think their moral standards are worse than mine. Nor are mine worse than theirs because I disagree with them. Whether I am a socialist or a believer in free enterprise, a philosophical anarchist or a believer in strong government, is a matter not of conscience but of economic and political belief. Reasonable men with the same high goals in mind can disagree over such matters. Accordingly, the questions that I think Mr. Zinn has raised are questions elaborately beside the point. My own view is that he is throwing dust in your eyes and playing to the primitive instinct in you. Now I say this with some passion, and I usually am considered cool. But I am not going to accept a show of more passion on issues on which I feel passion, too. One thing that I feel very passionate about is getting an answer to a question I never get when I hear the statement made that what is wrong with the world is that the wrong people are in power and the right people are out of power. Plato said it, it has been said by the prophets, I say it every morning when I read the newspapers, and I know who the right people are —they are me and my friends, me and the people who think as I do. Now, my question is, By what public procedure, what procedure that shows a fair and decent respect for other individuals, shall we decide who are the right people and who are the wrong people? By what procedure shall we decide who should go to jail and who should not? It is not an answer to say that the system we now have makes mistakes. It does indeed. The question is, What do you propose that would be better? I can propose some changes that would improve matters, but one thing that I would never think of proposing is that the decision as to who should be punished should be left to me and my friends. It should *not* be left to me and those of us who take the same political views I happen to hold. It is perfectly true, as Mr. Zinn says, that the first amendment said the Congress should not abridge freedom of speech, and that in seven or eight years there was Congress doing just that. But why should I trust Mr. Zinn to behave any better if he and the people he calls "the people" took power? Why should I trust myself? I think that I'm a well-intentioned man—as, I'm sure, most people think that they are well-intentioned—but I wouldn't trust myself any farther than I could see me if I were given the power to decide, without control by others, just who should be in jail and who shouldn't. I would like to think that I would withstand the temptations that others have not; even so, I don't think it would be good policy to give me this opportunity to test my fortitude. And I would certainly wonder whether a man had sufficient sense of the complexities of power, and the complexities in himself, to warrant giving him a blank check to make that sort of decision if he stood before a crowd and, speaking about the United States, just told them, with no ifs and buts, that "we all know everything is wrong—all wrong."

There are students in America who have done things much worse than students in the Soviet Union or Czechoslovakia. Since the question of jail has been brought up, where are these foreign students? Where are the Americans? It is unseemly, it is callous to overlook the fact that, with all the manifest evils in the United States, Martin Luther King is a national hero. It is unseemly to overlook the fact that Mr. Zinn is debating freely with me and I have no advantages over him, except, of course, as I said, that I am right. Those who have a few good things can get complacent. It is very dangerous to get complacent, to think we have a lot because we have a little. But man is a fierce and dangerous animal. If you don't believe it, look into the eye of the next man who tries to convert you. There is no way of getting that animal to heaven. Certainly don't just trust him, any more than he would trust you. The man who says "Let us all disobey the state; it doesn't make any difference cause the state is naturally wrong" imagines that the state isn't made up of people. And he imagines, of course, that he and his friends are angels. This isn't an answer to a single problem. It is an evasion of every problem. It isn't the assertion of a superior morality; it is a refusal to make moral discriminations. I am sorry I wasn't as amusing as Mr. Zinn in my paper, but the reason was quite simple. Moral discrimination is a rational affair, it isn't a matter of just appealing to people's guts. In a university forum, I take it that my effort to remind you that reasoning, and making distinctions, and qualifying one's judgments are necessay and desirable will not be regarded as wholly out of place.

MR. ZINN replies: Now I have appealed to people's primitive instincts and Mr. Frankel has appealed to their rationality. There was a time when in a university setting you would think he had all the advantage. But something has happened in the university. Primitive instincts have somehow become important forces. *That is very good.* The traditional rationality of the university has always been myopic and limited. It is the primitive instincts of people who live closer to the crush of events that has always reminded the cool and rational people in the university of what the facts of life are. Rationality pretends to something that it doesn't have, a more accurate perception of the truth. But you cannot have this until you begin, just even *begin*, to sense and feel the world the way Jackson feels it in Soledad prison or the way the peasants feel it in Vietnam. It takes, I concede, some very delicate and artistic combinations of rationality and primitive feeling to begin to assess what is happening in the world and what we should do about it.

Mr. Frankel has predicated a good part of his assault—no, I shouldn't say that, his argument—on the notion that I think it is a matter of changing men, that there are wrong men in office and that we—I and my buddies—are the right men, and they are evil and we are good, and when we get in things will be okay. That is not what I said. I didn't even discuss that. That is not even beside my point. I think that the problem is changing men *and changing institutions.* We know that this is important, because it doesn't matter what men you put in the police force— good men, bad men, kind men, sweet men, sour men, brutal men —you put them in a police force and they begin to act the way policemen do. Whatever the psychological scale says about the various soldiers in the My Lai massacre, and they were psychologically different, they behaved pretty much the same way. Now there is a real problem in beginning to create a set of institutions which will induce people to behave in a different way, which will make it easier for the best in people to come forward. This involves, again, a very subtle and delicate and simultaneous change in institutions and in people's thinking. And it is not all one or the other.

That is why civil disobedience is important, because there is no such thing as the right persons getting into power. As soon as the right persons get into power you'd better get civilly disobedient. The nature of the state as it has been so far, which is a monopolization of power—or if you want to get pluralistic, an oligopolization of power—is such as to turn men, whoever they are, whatever their individuality, to the same pursuits. It all somehow comes out the same way. Whether you have Truman or Eisenhower or Kennedy or Johnson or Nixon in office we follow the same policies in Vietnam. Whoever occupies offices in the Department of Defense and the Department of State, their sensibilities somehow all get blended into that great machine.

So, no, that is not my point about men and the wrong people and the right people and what procedures should we use and what kind of society should we have. When you focus attention on the fact that people are bad and that you can't really trust people— and you look around and people are not angels—there is just enough truth to this to make us very circumspect about trusting ourselves or trusting movements for change. What that does is cause us to place more faith in the existing institutions. Mr. Frankel is right, existing institutions are run by men, and if you take the kind of men created by the institutions and put them at the helm of these institutions you have a frightful combination. What I'm saying is that what we have in the way of the decision-making process in the world and in the United States today is so horrendous as to cause us to begin to work very hard—knowing all the difficulties, knowing where all the weaknesses of people are—at beginning to create new institutions, new relationships, pockets of living with people beginning to show signs of another society until there are so many pockets around that you even begin to have a new society.

john w. gardner

10

THE NATIONAL CITIZENS' LOBBY:

A THIRD FORCE

Introduction: The relatively new techniques of survey research produced during the Eisenhower era a rather dismal view of the American voter. According to the pollsters, most voters were poorly informed about even the basic political issues. They were also ideologically

John W. Gardner served as Secretary of Health, Education, and Welfare from 1965 to 1968, when he resigned to become chairman of the National Urban Coalition and, in 1970, Common Cause. A native of California and a graduate of Stanford University, he received his Ph.D. in psychology in 1938 from the University of California at Berkeley and has taught at Connecticut College for Women and Mount Holyoke College. A marine during World War II, he joined the Carnegie Corporation in 1946 and became its president in 1955. His publications include *Excellence* (New York: Harper & Row, 1961); *Self-renewal: The Individual and the Innovative Society* (New York: Harper & Row, 1964); and *The Recovery of Confidence* (New York: W. W. Norton, 1970).

169

unsophisticated, and they were loyal to their party less because of what is represented than because they had inherited it from their parents. Slightly less than half were Democrats, slightly more than a third were Republicans. But the "normal" Democratic majority did not always prevail because Republicans had a better record of showing up at the polls on election day; because many Democrats, especially in the South, were unhappy with their party's national image; and because such national heroes as General Eisenhower were attractive to all voters. But more depressing to the survey researchers than the partisans' low level of information and poor turnout was the small size (roughly 20 percent) and poor record of the independents, who tended to be even more ill-informed than the partisan majority and yet who frequently provided the margin of victory. The virtue of this otherwise rather uninspiring constellation, however, was its relative stability.

More recent research, however, indicates that the tenacity of party loyalty is loosening markedly and that the independents are increasing both in numbers and in sophistication, especially among young voters. The once dominant Roosevelt coalition is coming unglued and the American political universe seems to be in a process of disintegration. Whereas it once generally pitted the Republican top of the socioeconomic pyramid against the Democratic bottom, thereby roughly balancing wealth against numbers, its new and as yet undetermined structure may align the top and the bottom against the middle—in the metropolis, the suburban elites and the ghetto poor against the hard hats—in a dangerous political milieu of great instability and high emotional content.

John W. Gardner is alarmed about a growing "sense of helplessness" which constitutes an "explosive charge that could splinter our two major parties . . . could lead us to follow the shallowest demagogues . . . could result in massive refusals to vote . . . [and] lead to increasing violence or to severe repressive measures." In response to this growing malaise, to the frustrations that flow from "a system without access," he summons us to rally to Common Cause—a national citizens' lobby that is billed as a third force, not a third party. Yet can such a nonpartisan group in the long run lobby effectively without also electing—that is, without rewarding its friends and posing credible threats to its enemies by granting or withholding votes and money to candidates; without, in effect, becoming partisan or becoming a third party? And what has been the fate of third parties in America? Eugene McCarthy, no stranger to maverick, independent politics, once dismissed Common Cause as an organization "without a past or a future and [with] a dubious present." Yet John Gardner testifies below to its goals and its promising beginnings, and his testimony reflects at once not only our national crisis of confidence but also our historic legacy of enduring, if sorely beset, optimism as well.

ANYONE WHO HAS FOLLOWED contemporary discussions of violence is thoroughly familiar with two widely expressed theses: (1) that violence stems *in part* from social frustration and (2) that the alternative to violence is to work within the system. Neither assertion has proven very comforting, because no one has had much luck in coping with the social frustrations, and working within the system has yielded few brilliant solutions lately. Why? Why are we so frustrated? Is it possible to work within the system?

As a nation we have never faced more ominous problems— the threat of nuclear war, irreversible destruction of the environment, a world population crisis, urban decay, civil disorder. I don't need to elaborate about the seriousness of those issues. The reader has seen these problems growing steadily in scope and intensity, and he has seen also our apparently increasing inability to gain command of our problems. I travel constantly—in every part of this country—and I find everywhere, among all segments of the populace, something approaching a sense of helplessness. They hardly know how to begin.

In my judgment there is only one way to begin and that is to repair and renew and redesign our political and governmental institutions. Those institutions have fallen into serious disrepair, and until we overhaul them we shall not accomplish any significant public purposes. I do not make that statement lightly. I have spent the past five years working intensively on problems of poverty, discrimination, education, health, housing, employment, and so on. That work has taken me into federal agencies, state legislatures, city councils, the Congress of the United States, and every other part of the public process. And I can tell you that we will not solve any of the substantive problems I mentioned until we repair the instrumentalities by which we accomplish our shared purposes, namely our political and governmental institutions.

I hasten to say that we have ourselves to blame for the decay of the public process. The American citizen has paid virtually no serious attention to his political and governmental institutions. It is ironic that a people who would fight and die for the principle of self-government neglect the instruments of self-government, but that is just what we have done. As a result, our political and governmental institutions are in grave need of overhaul. City government, state government, the Congress of the United States, federal regulatory agencies, the courts, the political parties—all are in serious need of attention. They are poorly designed for contemporary purposes. They are not responsive to our will. They create rather than solve problems. They waste taxpayers' money. And worst of all, they make it impossible for good men to be effective in public life. The system smothers such men, thwarts them, chews them up. Contrary to the popular impression, good men *do* go into politics and government. I have seen them go into Congress, into city councils, into state legislatures—and the results are depressing. They find themselves hamstrung, caught in antiquated institutions that cannot be made to function effectively.

It is not a question of efficiency for efficiency's sake. Government and politics in a free society will never be genuinely efficient. But when our political and governmental institutions are no longer responsive, when they can no longer be held accountable, then we all suffer. We spend billions to solve our problems and fail to solve them. We support vast and intricate public machinery that does not in fact serve human needs. I believe that the American people are sufficiently troubled to be ready to take corrective action.

In every part of this country, I find—among working people, executives, minority groups, middle class housewives, young people, old people—the same troubled mood. There is a feeling that things aren't working. There is profound skepticism about our political and governmental processes. There is disillusionment with the two major parties. Such feelings constitute a kind of explosive charge that could splinter our two major parties. It could lead us to follow the shallowest of demagogues. It could result in massive refusals to vote. It could lead to increasing violence or to severe repressive measures.

But that same electric charge might be the fuel for a truly constructive movement. The very depth and breadth of concern means that many people are ready to act constructively even if it means sacrifice. I think one can already see the beginnings of a powerful movement to call the great institutions of our society to account. There is in virtually all segments and classes of society today a feeling that the institutions that should be serving us aren't serving us, that we are powerless before the vastness and complexity of our own society and before the giant institutions that stand astride our national life. Given that concern, it is not surprising to see a variety of groping efforts to bring our ruling institutions, corporate and governmental, back to some reasonable accountability. The ombudsman concept is being tried in various places. Young lawyers are using litigation in various ingenious ways to call private and public agencies to account. Consumerism, which is so far largely a middle class phenomenon, is essentially the same kind of effort.

The new politics and the politics of protest offer some innovative ways in which citizens can needle the great institutions of our society and demand an accounting of them. But as the movement continues, the American citizen is going to make a startling discovery. He is going to find that most of the new techniques for citizen action pale to insignificance before the enormous unused potential of the instruments of self-government that the citizen has allowed to grow rusty and out of repair. Until he turns again to those instruments, scrapes away the rust, repairs them and resharpens them, perhaps even redesigns them, he will not regain command of his society. And what are those instruments? They are precisely the city councils, the state legislatures, the political parties, the federal agencies, and other institutions that the American citizen has neglected for so long. Fortunately, the deterioration of the public process is reversible. Human institutions can be overhauled and renewed. We can make government accountable. We can make political processes serve our purposes.

The solutions are not mysterious. Any good city councilman, state legislator, party official, or member of Congress can tell you highly practical steps that might be taken tomorrow to make the system more responsive. But there has been no active, powerful, hard-hitting constituency to fight for such steps. It was to provide just that kind of constituency that some of us created the new national citizens' lobby known as Common Cause.

Institutions don't overhaul themselves. They resist renewal. They find it painful. When an institution grows rigid and unresponsive, someone must shake it up. And in the case of political and governmental institutions, the shakeup must come from concerned citizens determined to create responsive government, determined to bring the parties to life, determined to cut through organizational dry rot and revitalize aging institutions. That is what Common Cause is about.

Common Cause is a national citizens' lobby. We will lobby in the public interest at all levels of government, but especially at the federal level. We will assist our members to speak and act in behalf of legislation designed to solve the nation's problems. We will press for a reordering of national priorities. We will also press for the revitalization of the public process, to make our political and governmental institutions more responsive to the needs of the nation and the will of its citizens. We will uphold the public interest against all comers—special interests, self-seeking politicians, self-perpetuating bureaucrats, industry, professional groups. And we will uphold the interest of the individual American when it is put in hazard by the vast and complex institutions that dominate our national life.

Sophisticated observers of our national life doubt the effectiveness of idealistic citizen action, but the historical record on that point isn't as discouraging as they imply. As Wallace Sayre put it, "People say 'You can't fight city hall,' but in fact someone is always fighting city hall and often winning." In terms of national action, relatively small groups of crusading citizens won the vote for women, abolished child labor, launched the conservation movement, forced us to care about retarded children, and so on. Before 1969 the organized conservation movement consisted of no more than 200,000 or 300,000 citizens. But they won allies among editors, writers, congressmen, opinion makers—and they pushed the environmental issue to the top of the national agenda. That kind of citizen action has a long tradition in our national life, and those who don't grasp its impact have missed an important feature of this society. I not only believe it has been effective in the past, I believe it can be made vastly *more* effective. And I regard it as a mistake to see such citizen action as something outside the political process. It is an integral part of the political process just as special interest lobbying is a part of the political process.

Common Cause is a third force, not a third party. We will urge each of our members to join the party of his choice. More important, we will urge him to be active and to make his party a more responsive part of our political machinery. Common Cause itself will not support political candidates. It will confine itself to issues. We have a governing board of seventy men and women drawn from every segment of American life. It includes business leaders, minority group leaders, mayors, religious leaders, labor leaders, educators, governors, and so on. We are now designing arrangements whereby members will also be given a voice in governing the organization.

We will rely on well-established techniques of bringing citizen opinion to bear on legislative issues. We have had extensive experience in citizen action through our predecessor organization, the Urban Coalition Action Council. In its three years of intensive and successful activity at the federal level, the council worked with a variety of allies—civil rights organizations, religious groups, the business community, the labor community—and participated in major legislative victories. So we know from first-hand experience that citizen action can be effective. But we can't possibly function effectively until we have a large membership, so the first thing we have asked members to do is to recruit other members. We don't want a slow rate of growth that brings us substantial membership two years from now—we want it now because we want to be effective now.

The second thing we will ask members to do is the kind of homework that will make them effective in citizen action. They should know all they can learn about their congressman. They ought to know what his stated positions are, what actions he has taken, what his strengths and weaknesses are. They should have the same knowledge of their two senators, their governor, and their state legislators. We will help them do their homework. We will keep them up to date on important issues before the Congress and we will let them know what they might do, at any given time, to influence those issues.

Next, we hope to persuade our members to become active in their own communities. They can do something about the quality of life in their city. They can do something about their schools. We will help them find the points of leverage. The goal is to produce a body of active, interested, engaged citizens who will work in every possible way to make this a better country.

Many people today are interested in new strategies for citizen action; and so are we—but first things first. As Vince Lombardi said, "First learn to block and tackle." A citizen must understand the processes of self-government. He must learn to use intelligently the instruments that are available to him. His capacity to make his views felt at the federal level is particularly important. The public interest can be benefited or butchered by the day-to-day decisions of federal agencies or actions of Congress.

We are still in the process of developing our agenda, in collaboration with our governing board and our members. But we know the general direction in which we intend to go. We must end the war. We must bring about a drastic change in national priorities. We must renew our attack on poverty and discrimination. We must seek far-reaching solutions in housing, employment, education, health, family planning, environment, income maintenance, consumer protection, transportation, law enforcement, and the administration of justice.

But behind and beneath those issues—and more fundamental than those issues—is the repair of the public process which I discussed earlier. Until we tackle that problem we'll never get at the substantive problems of housing, employment, education, and all the rest. Obviously, we cannot expect that the members of Common Cause will be in agreement among themselves on all issues. If our organization is a lively one, full of vital people, there will be lots of disagreement. But the public opinion polls show that there are a surprising number of issues on which a high percentage of Americans agree. They all want decent housing. Even the middle class is suffering from high rents that stem from the housing shortage. Most Americans want good schools. Most

Americans want constructive employment programs. Most are concerned for a healthy and stable economy. All want effective law enforcement and efficient administration of justice. We don't expect every member of Common Cause to agree with every detail of our agenda. But our policy council has learned in three years of experience that it is possible to take significant positions that will be agreed on by Americans of widely differing backgrounds.

Of course many observers believe that "the people," that is, individual Americans, are powerless before the great interlocking machinery of our society. Such observers believe that we have to accomplish a shift of power. But power is the capacity to influence the course of events. The reason citizens have lost that capacity is that they have allowed *their* instruments of power—the instruments of self-government—to fall into disrepair. So when they turn to government for effective pollution control or consumer protection legislation, government fails them. When they seek effective administration of justice, the courts fail them. When they seek excellent candidates for public office, the parties fail them. It is *only* by regaining command of the instruments of self-government and making those instruments effective that the people will regain command of their situation.

A word about special interests and the public interest is in order here. It was once widely believed that "interest group pluralism" would solve all of our problems. Each special interest may act selfishly (so the argument went), but all of them taken together balance each other out so that the public interest and the interest of individual Americans is served. The trouble is, it isn't true. Interest group pluralism has accounted for a good deal of our dynamism as a nation, but it has clear limitations. Let us preserve it, let us expect that it will serve us in important ways, but let us not imagine that it will do all the things that need to be done. Too often the public interest and the interests of the ordinary individual simply fall between the stools of the interest groups. We need them, but we also need a strong, effective voice for the public interest.

The initial response to Common Cause has far exceeded our expectations. It has been extraordinary in both quality and quantity. In less than half a year we attracted a membership of more than 100,000 members. And that brings me to one final question. How will we know, and when will we know, whether Common Cause is a success or failure?

We will be able to make a short-term judgment in one or two years. The questions to ask will be: How active are our members? Have we increased their effectiveness in citizen action? Have we changed anything? How many legislative victories do we have to our credit? But we are less interested in that short-term judgment than in long-term goals. We're after bigger game than a few legislative victories. We would regard Common Cause as a long-term success if five years from now it had brought about a recognition on the part of the American people that they must apply the same philosophy of repair and redesign to their political institutions that they apply to every other part of life. Nothing stands still. You can't neglect anything and expect that it will remain alive and functioning. This society is facing profound changes. Our political institutions must be equal to that challenge. That requires a vital, alive, concerned attention to those institutions. If Common Cause can persuade the American people as a matter of habit to give creative attention to their public institutions, I would regard that as an important mark of success.

Second, we hope to bring about a sharp increase in the number of good men who go into public life. Many good men spurn public life today. When this nation began in the 1770s it had a population of about 3 million, roughly the present population of Los Angeles. Yet it produced at least a dozen statesmen of extraordinary quality—men with an exceptional gift for leadership, men capable of the highest order of statecraft, men with intellectual gifts and a capacity for action. Surely today, with sixty times greater population, we must have far more men and women of that caliber in our population. We must have many potential Jeffersons, Madisons, Franklins, and Hamiltons. But where are they? For the most part they simply do not enter public life, and those who do find themselves trapped in institutions that cannot be made to function effectively.

Urban violence is only one among many symptoms of a society wracked by conflict, a society torn by the ever-increasing tempo of change, a society that must at all costs regain command of itself. The only way to accomplish that is to overhaul our political and governmental institutions. We had better get on with it.

THE JOHNS HOPKINS PRESS

Designed by Victoria Dudley

Composed in Times Roman text and display
by Monotype Composition Company

Bound in Columbia Fictionette
by Moore and Company, Inc.

Printed on 60-lb. Sebago MF, Regular
by The Murray Printing Company